Praise for *Teachers Who Change Lives*:

'I love this book. It is the first book I have ever read that accurately depicts the mystery and power of the relationship between a passionate teacher and a responsive student … This book explains the love that lies at the heart of successful teaching and the dynamics of a life-changing educational relationship. The personal stories are both inspirational and full of practical advice.'

Julie McCrossin, journalist and broadcaster

'Good teachers do a great deal more than simply impart information—they encourage, inspire and help the ... 'ents gain knowledge about the subjects they study, about the ... and about themselves. Everyone has a story of a teacher who in ... enced his or her life—for better or worse. Metcalfe and Game have ... mined the memories of well-known Australians and juxtaposed these with the reflections of passionate educators. The result is an invaluable resource for beginning teachers looking for guidance about how to develop productive classroom relationships.'

Roslyn Guy, *The Age*

'In *Teachers Who Change Lives*, Andrew Metcalfe and Ann Game tell vivid stories of Australian teachers and their impact, sometimes from the teachers' own point of view and sometimes from their pupils' recollections later in life. Woven through these stories is a beautifully written reflection on teaching and learning, which rightly emphasises that the centre of it all is a living relationship between teacher and learner.

The authors offer firm opinions on what is and is not good teacher strategy, which will certainly arouse debate. Yet I think all concerned with Australian education will welcome their lively accounts of classrooms that work effectively, teachers who have insight into what is really needed by their pupils, and pupils who respond with unexpected moments of insight and new pleasure in learning. It is good to read a warm-hearted and intelligent account of education working well.'

R. W. Connell
Professor of Education
University of Sydney

TEACHERS WHO CHANGE LIVES

TEACHERS WHO CHANGE LIVES

Andrew Metcalfe and Ann Game

MELBOURNE
UNIVERSITY
PRESS

MELBOURNE UNIVERSITY PRESS
An imprint of Melbourne University Publishing Limited
187 Grattan Street, Carlton, Victoria 3053, Australia
mup-info@unimelb.edu.au
www.mup.com.au

First published 2006
Text © Andrew Metcalfe and Ann Game 2006
Design and typography © Melbourne University Publishing Ltd 2006

Designed by Nada Backovic Designs
Typeset in Bembo 10.8/14 point by Syarikat Seng Teik Sdn. Bhd., Malaysia
Printed in Australia by McPherson's Printing Group

National Library of Australia Cataloguing-in-Publication entry:

Metcalfe, Andrew W. (Andrew William).
    Teachers who change lives.

    Includes index.
    ISBN 978 0 52285 175 5.
    ISBN 0 522 85175 4.

    1. Teachers—Australia—Attitudes. 2. Teacher effectiveness—Australia.
    3. Motivation in education. 4. Teacher–student relationships—Australia.
    I. Game, Ann. II. Title.

371.110994

CONTENTS

I love that bird who put wings on my feet. I didn't become a
flying creature by my own efforts—far from it—it was thanks to
him that I was able to pass ... into this vast new world.
So we feel a special gratitude to these extraordinary pedagogues
who make it possible for us to enter new worlds.
Michel Serres, 1995: 162

The teachers I had were just marvellous and I owe a lot to them.
Next to your parents, teachers have the greatest influence on
your mind expansion. Certainly they did in my case. ... I'll
always be grateful to my teachers. I remember them like a rosary
(even though I'm Anglican). I go through them seriatim. I go
through each one of them. I remember each one of them quite
vividly. They're not forgotten in my mind. They're clattering
around in my brain. They were great influences in my life.
Michael Kirby

PREFACE

Although the problems in education are endlessly debated, we seldom hear about what goes on when teaching is at its best. Educational policies are in the public domain, but the classroom is a private place. This book hopes to redress this imbalance. Based on stories about teachers who have changed lives, it makes public the ongoing, unexpressed gratitude that many people feel for their teachers. By reflecting on these stories, we hope to raise awareness of the attributes and needs of good teaching.

Parents, teachers and students are vitally interested in what makes the difference between good and bad teaching: What do teachers do to make a class inspiring? What do they do to bring out the best in students? These are understandable questions—we ask them of ourselves after disappointing classes, parents ask them when considering their children's futures. Nevertheless these questions are misleading if they assume that teaching is the responsibility of the teacher alone. Teaching is not simply a matter of transmitting knowledge from one to another; it cannot be reduced to inputs and outputs of teacher and student. Rather, teaching and learning are the transformations brought through unique and living relationships. Because relationships happen *between* people, both teachers and students are teaching and learning. If this does not occur, the teacher's lessons cannot meet the particular needs of each student.

What we bring to discussions of teaching and education is this sociological appreciation of social relations. Relational logic makes a decisive difference to how we think about the basic concepts used to describe teaching and learning experiences, concepts like interest, facilitation, dialogue, modelling, feedback, enthusiasm, engagement, authority and trust. When these terms take on their richer relational meanings, we can avoid the stand-offs that characterise current educational debates.

These debates typically turn on abstract oppositions: Is education too focused on learning or too focused on teaching? Does the teacher's concern with pastoral care distract them from the curriculum? Do teachers have too much authority or students too much freedom? Whereas such questions presume an either/or answer, a relational perspective shows that these apparent oppositions are two sides of the same coin. In the real life of the best classrooms, we find that learning and teaching presuppose each other, as do care and the curriculum, authority and freedom.

This book, therefore, takes a step aside from current debates and returns to the most basic everyday issues: How does learning happen? What goes on between teachers and students in an effective classroom? How do students learn the values that underlie a good life? Every day, in ordinary classrooms, learning brings the delight of life to countless students. This sense of wonder occurs not despite, but through life's vicissitudes.

To explore the relation between teacher and student, we interviewed people from a diversity of fields. We spoke to teachers of maths, languages, sciences, humanities, art, theatre, music and sport, teachers from all levels of formal education, teachers just beginning their careers, and teachers who came to our attention because of their reputations for excellence. To collect stories from the student's perspective, we interviewed well-known Australians and asked them to explain the roles that teachers have played in their lives. Finally, to round out our understanding, we spoke to parents of schoolchildren.

Although our interviews focused on particular teachers in particular situations, what emerged was the universality of good teaching. A sporting coach and a kindergarten teacher espouse the same principles as Socrates and Thomas Aquinas. To give a sense of how we address these universal themes, here is a description of each chapter.

Changing Lives without Aiming to

Inspiring teachers always challenge students, but they do not set out to shape them and do not know how or when to measure the success of their classes. Through the strange chemistry of class-room relations, students change and yet become more themselves.

Seeing Potential in Students

Good teaching recognises the unique potential of each student. This is not the same as an expectation or a prediction; it is seeing students in their wholeness, as they are now. The teacher's respon-sibility is to nurture students and draw out their potential by open-ing them to new worlds. Thus teaching is inherently ethical, allowing students to find their place in and to contribute to the world.

Teaching as a Form of Love

Teachers can see potential only when the teaching relationship is characterised by love and respect. Whereas desire is partial, because it is self-centred, pedagogic love keeps teachers and students open-minded, patient and respectful of differences. There is no conflict between the teacher's duty to care and their duty to teach because care is at the heart of the teaching relation. Teachers can teach a love of learning, a love of a discipline, a love of life, only if they love teaching.

A Passion for Learning

Although students remember the passion of their teachers, the vitality of the classroom is an energy that teachers and students produce together. The successful teacher must be able to receive, if they are to be able to give. Because this energy isn't flowing in one direction, passion has the undistracted stillness that learning requires.

The Importance of Authority

While teachers cannot make students learn, they can create the situation where learning happens. They provide students with the trustworthy order that allows them to set aside their fears and engage in the openness of the learning process. This order arises from a responsive rather than an externally imposed authority; rather than restricting students, it draws them out. Students recognise the teacher's authority because teachers orientate it to the needs of students.

The Process of Learning

Teachers create a situation where students can unselfconsciously engage in learning. This is an open-hearted and playful process where students find themselves in the discipline, as they find the discipline in themselves. It is this feel for a discipline that allows students to receive their teacher's technical knowledge.

Dialogue as an Opening of the Mind

Although commonly mistaken as an exchange of views, dialogue is a pedagogic process in which new ways of thinking emerge *between* people. The teacher's skill lies in modelling the ethics of openness: they hold their knowledge until students call for it; when they ask questions, they are ready to learn from the answers; rather than instructing, the teachers listen to students and feed back challenging questions.

Playing Your Part

The canon doesn't restrict student self-expression but develops it: students find their particularity by taking part in the life of cultural traditions. Because a tradition is continually changing, teachers initiate students to its wonders by allowing students to show them these wonders in a new light. In this way, teachers demonstrate to students that the tradition will carry them if they carry it.

A Full Life

Contrary to the common view that education is a preparation for adulthood and real life, maturity, from a relational view, is a capacity for the ongoing learning of open relationship. In particular, this involves the ability to have a reflexive relation with yourself, to be both teacher and student. Life-changing teachers remain with us as guiding spirits that connect us to life.

ACKNOWLEDGEMENTS

First of all, we want to thank our generous interviewees: Stephanie Alexander, Diana Borinski, Linda Burnett, Dawn Casey, Greg Chappell, Sharon Cheers, Betty Churcher, Anna Clark, Paul Cudmore, Ann Daniel, Leslie Devereaux, Barbara Devlin, Diana Doherty, Anna Eggert, Raimond Gaita, Eddie Game, Elizabeth Game, Tom Game, Helen Garner, Shane Gould, Guy Hungerford, Nick Jose, Cath Kevin, Lesley King, Michael Kirby, Kym Lawry, Julie McCrossin, Drusilla Modjeska, Judith Moreland-Mitchell, Bruce Nuske, Jenny Oliver, Josie Pellicane, Veronica Quinteros, David Ritchie, Vilma Rotellini, Karen Tinney, Vicky Yannakouros and John Yu. All helped us clarify our understanding of the educational process, but the interpretations of the interviews are our responsibility.

Unless otherwise indicated, the quotations in the book are based on tape-recorded interviews. Because of a technical problem recording Raimond Gaita's interview, however, we have relied on two conference papers (2001, 2004) that deal with the main story he told us. With Betty Churcher's permission, we have supplemented her interview in a couple of places with details she gave in an interview with Peter Thompson (2004).

We would like to thank people who helped us establish and carry out the project. These include Jo Fraser, Elizabeth Game, Tim Game, Cath Kevin, Drusilla Modjeska and Zora Simic.

We are grateful for support from Adrian Lee and Michele Scoufis, two people passionate about the promotion of learning and teaching at the University of New South Wales.

We want to thank the friends and family members who have supported us while we've written this book, especially Anita, Leo and Max Sibrits; Alison Clark and Libby Silva; and the Metcalfe, Sibrits and Game families.

Finally, we would like to express gratitude to Paul Alexander, Mr Hughes, Mrs Lindsay, Alastair MacLachlan, Mrs Smith; Diana Bowman, Graeme Duncan, Helen Kay. This book is dedicated to all our teachers.

THE STUDENTS AND TEACHERS

While researching this book, we heard many more interesting stories than we could use in the final text: not all our interviewees are quoted, and while some people appear throughout the book, some make only one appearance. Because we have sought to preserve a sense of the particular voice and personality of each interviewee, readers may be curious to know more about them. Here are biographical notes provided by the students and teachers who are quoted. Parents preferred not to be named in the text so we have not included notes on them.

STUDENTS

Stephanie Alexander is Australia's foremost food writer. For twenty-one years her restaurant Stephanie's was regarded as an essential Melbourne experience, and she was a founding partner in the Richmond Hill Cafe and Larder. Stephanie is increasingly involved in the Kitchen Garden at Collingwood College, a project that allows primary school children to learn about food by growing it, harvesting it and sharing it at the table. She was awarded an Order of Australia in 1994 for her services to the hospitality industry and to tourism, and for encouraging young apprentices.

Dawn Casey is known internationally for her work as the Director of the National Museum of Australia. She was responsible for the construction and development of the museum, which opened as a Centenary of Federation project in 2001. Other achievements have included her major contributions to Indigenous policies and programs, to Australia's Cultural Heritage and to AusAID. She serves on numerous national bodies, particularly those relating to cultural, educational and Indigenous affairs. She has won many public service medals and has twice been awarded honorary doctorates. Dawn is currently CEO of the Western Australian Museum.

Greg Chappell played eighty-seven test matches and captained Australia forty-eight times. He retired from test cricket in January 1984 as the batsman with the highest number of runs in Australian test history. Since his retirement, Greg has served as a member of the Australian Cricket Board, as coach at state and national levels, as an Australian cricket selector and as a cricket commentator. Greg is also a best-selling author with his health, lifestyle and cricket books. His latest book, *The Making of Champions*, is based on his research into the cricket champions from Bradman to the present day. In 1979, Greg was awarded an MBE, and in 2003 an Australian Centenary Medal.

Betty Churcher was born in 1931 in Brisbane. Art has always been her private and public passion. As an educator, gallery director, television presenter and writer, her vision is to make people see art as accessible and relevant. While Director of the National Gallery of Australia from 1990 to 1997, she oversaw both its widening public appeal and its rise as an institution of cultural significance, locally and internationally. The first female director of the gallery, Betty has been a role model for women for many years. She became the first woman director of a state art gallery when appointed to the Art Gallery of Western Australia in 1987. In 1982, she was the first female head of a tertiary institution as Dean of the School of Art and Design at Melbourne's Phillip Institute of Technology.

Diana Doherty was born in Brisbane and began studying violin, piano and oboe at primary school, later focusing on oboe. As a student, both in Australia and overseas, Diana won many prestigious awards and prizes, including the Prague Spring Festival Competition of 1991. Since then, she has toured extensively as a soloist, most recently playing with the New York Philharmonic, conducted by Lorin Maazel. Diana joined the Sydney Symphony Orchestra as Principal Oboe in 1997. She has released several CDs, and teaches oboe at the Sydney Conservatorium of Music.

Raimond Gaita was born in Germany in 1946 and migrated to Australia in 1950. He was educated at Baringhup Primary School, St Patrick's College Ballarat, Melbourne High School and the Universities of Melbourne and Leeds. He is Professor of Moral Philosophy at King's College, University of London, and Foundation Professor of Philosophy at Australian Catholic University. Raimond is best known to the general reader for his memoir, *Romulus, My Father*. He has written many other books, one of which, *Good and Evil: An Absolute Conception*, is dedicated to his teacher Martin Winkler. Raimond contributes extensively to public discussion about reconciliation, political morality, genocide, education and responses to terrorism.

Helen Garner taught in Victorian high schools until she was fired from the Education Department in 1972 and had to start writing for a living. Since then she has published novels and short stories, written screenplays, and worked as a freelance journalist and reviewer. Her books have won various literary prizes, and in 1993 she received a Walkley Award for feature journalism.

She now reviews movies for *The Monthly* magazine, and her most recent book is *Joe Cinque's Consolation*.

Shane Gould is still a household name many years after her triumphs at the 1972 Munich Olympics. The only person to hold every world freestyle record from 100 metres to 1500 metres simultaneously, and the only swimmer ever to win three Olympic Gold medals in world record time, she had a short but dramatic career. Shane's life has paralleled her swimming: it has been a series of tumble turns as she has undertaken new challenges. She has taught swimming, surfing and natural horsemanship, always setting high standards for technical accuracy. What is most important to her is the 'feel' in a sport: feel for the horse, feel of the water, feel of the ocean's power. This connection is, for Shane, a meditative thing, a practical outworking of her reverence for God and nature.

Nicholas Jose grew up in South Australia and has lived and worked in Britain, Italy, China and the United States. He has published short stories; essays; translations; several acclaimed novels including *Paper Nautilus*, *The Rose Crossing*, *The Custodians* and *The Red Thread*; and a memoir, *Black Sheep: Journey to Borroloola*. His most recent book is a novel, *Original Face*. He was Cultural Counsellor at the Australian Embassy, Beijing, 1987–90, and has written widely on contemporary Asian and Australian culture. He was president of Sydney PEN, 2002–2005. Nick currently holds the Chair of Creative Writing at the University of Adelaide.

Michael Kirby was born and educated in public schools in Sydney. He had an excellent education and is a strong proponent of the democratic values and egalitarianism of public schools. He was Foundation Chairman of the Australian Law Reform Commission (1975–84) and President of the NSW Court of Appeal

(1984–96) before his appointment to the High Court of Australia, the nation's supreme court. Michael has also served in international bodies, as President of the International Commission of Jurists and UN Special Representative in Cambodia, and he currently participates in the UNESCO International Bioethics Committee and the UNAIDS Panel on Human Rights. Through all of his work he seeks to reflect the values he learned in his schooling.

Julie McCrossin talks for a living. Until recently she presented *Breakfast* on 702 ABC Sydney, after five years on ABC Radio National's weekday morning show *Life Matters*. She is best known for her role as a team leader on the media quiz show *Good News Week* on ABC TV and Network Ten. Julie has worked as a children's entertainer in schools, child welfare institutions and prisons with the theatre-in-education group Pipi Storm, and as an adult literacy teacher for TAFE. She has also worked in community legal education with a focus on the rights of children and people with disabilities. Julie has qualifications in Arts, Education and Law.

Drusilla Modjeska taught writing at the University of Technology, Sydney between 1978 and 1989, when she left to focus on her own writing. Her books *Poppy*, *The Orchard* and *Stravinsky's Lunch* have each won major prizes. 'I am now running the thesis-to-book project at the University of Sydney, which has shown me a different form of teaching. The one-to-one way of working allows the relationship to grow in its own way and time. I am filled with awe at what these young people do. The results are always more than either of us could have imagined at the beginning.'

TEACHERS

Sharon Cheers, primary school teacher, has a passion for education and believes that working with young, curious minds is an honour. From the start of her career, she has been inspired by the sense of wonder and the desire to learn that children possess. Sharon is committed to developing classroom cultures where questions abound and student engagement is high. She enjoys planning programs that are rich with intellectual quality, allowing student thinking to be challenged and valued. As a teacher of ten years, Sharon has been a Special Needs teacher, Coordinator of Early Literacy and currently holds the position of Head of Curriculum, Kindergarten to Year 6. She has a Bachelor of Education (Primary) and a Masters of Education in the area of Teaching and Curriculum.

Leslie Devereaux, anthropology lecturer and psychotherapy supervisor, had a peripatetic childhood in America with her lesbian artist mother and grandmother. Her undergraduate and postgraduate education was at Harvard University, with several life-changing teachers. As an anthropologist, she lived for many years in Chiapas, Mexico and in Cape York, Queensland, and taught anthropology at the Australian National University for nearly twenty years. Her Zen teacher was Robert Aitken, Roshi. In more recent years she has trained as a Jungian analyst, taught by Russell Meares, Giles Clark, Anne Brown and Peter Fullerton. She practices in Canberra.

Barbara Devlin, high-school English teacher, gained her Postgraduate Certificate in Education at Hull University under Dr Robert Protherough, a leading light in English teaching. Barbara began her career at a mixed comprehensive school on the outskirts of Leeds, teaching English and Drama. She moved to Australia in 1992 planning to stay for two years. 'It was so fantastic, we stayed!' In 1998, Barbara moved to her current school where she is Assistant Head of English. 'The very humbling thankyou notes from students over the years make all those evenings of marking worth it!'

Anna Eggert, sculptor and art teacher, was born in Croatia in 1952, and her family migrated to Sydney in 1962. She studied history at Sydney University and completed a Dip. Ed. in Melbourne. Completing her Bachelor of Visual Art at the Canberra School of Art in 1991, she has been an artist ever since. Anna has had twelve solo shows, has been included in many group shows and has won or been a finalist in many prizes, including the National Sculpture Prize, Woollahra Small Sculpture Prize, the Alice Prize and the McClelland Award and Survey. Anna has worked as a teacher nearly all her working life.

Elizabeth Game, high-school English and legal studies teacher, had a country childhood and education. She studied Law and Arts, before travelling and working overseas. As her four children began their schooling, she recognised her own interest in education and returned to university to study teaching. In these 'mature age' studies, and later, in the classroom, Elizabeth found that her parenting experience and training in legal reasoning were enormously useful. She won the Australian College of Education (SA) Award for Excellence in Teacher Education Studies. As a parent, Elizabeth has taken an active role in school governance. She is currently a professional practice manager.

Guy Hungerford, sociology tutor, was born in Sydney in 1976. His primary and secondary education took place in Australia, Japan and England, at six different schools. He noticed at some point that a good class was one of the best things in life and a bad class one of the worst. At university he studied History, Economics and Sociology, the last of which became the field in which he did

Honours and commenced a PhD in the sociology of education. Guy has been a tutor for several years. He believes that good teaching should animate both the student's and the teacher's interest in the subject.

Kym Lawry, high-school physics and maths teacher, commenced teaching in 1989 in Port Lincoln, following the completion of a BSc (Honours, Physics) from the University of Adelaide and a Graduate Dip. Ed. from the South Australian College of Advanced Education. After two years in Port Lincoln and another year teaching in Adelaide, he undertook a year of travel, including three months' work experience and study with an Indian aid organisation in Delhi. Kym has been teaching at his current school for twelve years, with a one-year break as an Australian Volunteer Abroad in Western Samoa. He is the Head of Physics, and has acted as the Head of Science and the Assistant Head of the Senior School.

Judith Moreland-Mitchell, high-school English, Latin and classical studies teacher, did a BA and teaching training at the University of Sydney, and a Graduate Diploma in Educational Studies (Multicultural Education) at Armidale College of Advanced Education. 'Reflecting on my forty-year career, I realise that teaching is a vocation: from the moment I entered a classroom, I knew I had made the correct choice. I grew up when education was a privilege, not a right. That privilege brought its own responsibilities: to ensure that the emergent adults in my care would never abuse their intelligence and would leave my classes with a greater understanding of their world. I have never stopped being a student, undertaking many courses to expand my knowledge in my subject areas and beyond. I have contributed for many years to two State Curriculum Committees and am still the Chief Assessor of one.'

Jenny Oliver, primary school teacher, was born in Newcastle in 1970, and was inspired by her maths teacher to become a teacher herself. Jenny has taught in a variety of schools across New South Wales, and has been teaching in her current school in Sydney for five years. Her special interest is in art, and she is currently undertaking postgraduate studies to further her knowledge of the creative process. 'The real outcomes in teaching are always more than anyone could have predicted. The best moments are when students surprise themselves, and you, with what they can do.'

Josie Pellicane, primary school teacher, graduated from the University of Sydney in 1995. After travelling overseas, and working in fields outside teaching, she began her career in 1999, at the school where she still works. Josie has a strong interest in maths education and language learning, and has studied Italian, French and Cantonese. She is planning to learn Mandarin. 'I believe that a celebration of cultural diversity is a basic role of schooling.' Josie has taught across all grades from Kindergarten to Year 7 and, in 2003, she received a New South Wales Quality Teaching Award.

David Ritchie, actor, director and performance studies lecturer, completed his BA at the University of Natal, before going on to do honours degrees in English and Drama. Moving to Leeds, he did an MA in Theatre Studies. After teaching for a year in a high school, he was offered a scholarship to do a MPhil at Leeds. David took up a lectureship at Macquarie University where he is now Senior Lecturer in Critical and Cultural Studies. Throughout this time, David has continued to work at a professional level as a director, translator, actor and dramaturg. He has worked on new German-language productions, on Shakespearean productions, and on many new Australian works. In 1996, his production of *King Lear* won New Theatre's first Critics' Circle Award.

Vilma Rotellini, primary school teacher, has taught for twenty-five years, and is Head of the language department at her school. 'When I was younger I thought that I'd know all there was to teaching after a few years. Instead, I am learning and getting better at what I do year after year. My passion for teaching has grown. The pleasure I get when I see kids enjoying learning can be overwhelming. I love it when they are happy to come into my classroom not just to learn but because they want to be with each other and with me. As well as teaching subject matter, I want to incorporate into the teaching issues affecting everyday life, morals and values. I want students to respect and be respected, to love, care for and look out for each other. I want each child to be the best person they can be. Knowing that I have the opportunity to do this puts a smile on my face, it makes me feel that all is okay with the world.'

Vicky Yannakouros, primary school teacher, has taught for seventeen years, in Australia, Vietnam and Germany. In 2002, she won a New South Wales Quality Teaching Award. 'As my experience has grown, so has my passion for and understanding of what I do and why I do it. My foremost priority is for my children, to know that they are loved and valued as human beings. I want them to be open and giving as human beings, and open and inquisitive as learners. This underpins what I do every day in my classroom. Watching my children grow as human beings, the way they care for and support each other through good times and bad, is what brings tears to my eyes.'

CHAPTER ONE

CHANGING LIVES
WITHOUT AIMING TO

CHANGING LIVES

Helen Garner is one of Australia's most celebrated writers, with books ranging from *Monkey Grip* in 1977 to *Joe Cinque's Consolation* in 2004. How did Helen learn to write? Her primary school teacher taught her.

> Mrs Dunkley basically taught me everything I know about language, about the written word. I don't remember if we *read* anything in class. What she taught me was how to analyse sentences and how to construct them correctly. It was like being given the basic equipment for what I ended up doing. I feel very grateful to her for that.

Mrs Dunkley was strict and critical, 'on a hair trigger', and Helen generally felt incompetent at school. Mental arithmetic sessions left her with screaming nightmares. But Helen found delight in lessons on parsing and analysis. This was 'something I could do'. It had a beauty; 'it answered something for me'.

Helen remembered the moment that crystallised the significance of these classes. Mrs Dunkley was explaining adverbs to a generally uninterested Year 6 class, pointing out that adverbs modify both verbs and adjectives. Helen found herself asking a question, for one of the first times ever. She could understand how adverbs modify verbs, but how do they modify adjectives? Mrs Dunkley stopped and looked at Helen for a moment before answering the question.

> It was a terribly hot day, and I remember she looked at me and I just thought at that moment she looked at me as if— you know, looking back as a grown-up—I felt she looked at me with respect because I asked a question that showed that I was actually interested or that I was getting through to her. But I always remember that: asking about how could an adverb modify an adjective, and she gave an example *and I got it*. It was one of those moments of joy and learning.

The look that passed between them was a moment of surprise, of gratitude, of recognition, of respect, and perhaps affection. Whereas Mrs Dunkley's critical gaze pinned Helen down as incompetent, this look thrilled her with a sense of potential. She described the feeling as the joy of being on a train with others, surging forward together.

The moment Helen surprised herself was the moment she learned who she was. Amazed to see Mrs Dunkley's amazement, Helen must have realised that she had underestimated herself. She was capable of surprising others and herself, and this realisation was the basis of hope and self-respect. There were things she could do in life, even if she didn't know what they were. Perhaps this was when she was called to writing, though she couldn't have realised it at the time. The look lasted only a moment, but its unforgettable wonder remained.

Most of us can, like Helen, recall teachers who changed our lives. Certain teachers arrive to teach us just what we need to know, just when we need to know it. They are our path to knowledge. The amazing thing is not just that they change us, but that they change us so that we become ourselves. It's as if our meetings with them were foreordained, as if they have a magical ability to know us better than we know ourselves.

Helen's story reminds us how uncanny this life-changing process can be. It can occur in the most mundane gesture: a teacher looks at you, they lend you a book, they share a conversation with you in the schoolyard, they stay after hours to help you. The significance of this gesture may not be understood at the time, and throughout our lives we may constantly rediscover its meaning.

Disconcertingly, Helen's story also affirms that the teachers who have this effect are not necessarily like the saintly Mr Chips. Often students are afraid of the power of the teachers who mean most to them. Helen, for example, never grew to like Mrs Dunkley, though she 'now has only good feelings about her'. There is possibly something dark and certainly something awesome about the moments of learning when we discover who we are. Perhaps Helen trusted Mrs Dunkley's look—perhaps Mrs Dunkley's respect *got through* to Helen—because Mrs Dunkley had no illusions about Helen's weaknesses. Not all the life-changing teachers we heard about were as edgy as Mrs Dunkley, but all had this ability to see students as they really were.

STRANGE CHEMISTRY

Helen's story highlights the strange chemistry involved in good teaching. When teaching works, it isn't simply because teachers are kindly or knowledgeable. Effective learning and teaching rely on the connection manifest in Mrs Dunkley's look. When they connect with teachers, students are no longer who they thought they were: they change to become who they really are. To reveal the pattern of this curious transformation, here are three more archetypal stories of life-changing teachers. In each case, students turn into themselves through encounters with particular teachers.

Betty Churcher is best known for having made the National Gallery of Australia in Canberra more accessible during her time as its director. A faith in art's transformative powers has guided her whole career, as artist, teacher, curator, writer and broadcaster. Betty says that she owes this passion to her high school, which changed her life by introducing her to the world of art. Throughout her interview with us, Betty compared her vocation with that of her headmistress Miss Craig.

> I went to Somerville House and that to my mind was the great thing in my life, because it was an all-girls school, and that gave me a freedom of movement. The headmistress, Miss Craig, frightened the lives out of us. We called her the Vulture of Vulture Street. She swept around in her academic gown, catching girls who had been sent out of class—the most terrible thing that could happen to you if you'd been misbehaving. She was like God, always looming. But by gosh she was a huge influence in our lives. Miss Craig just had the magical ability of expecting the absolute best of us, no matter what it was. Whether we were going to be judges, brain surgeons or mothers, we had to do it to the very utmost of our ability, with 110 per cent of our concern, energy and wit.
>
> Although I didn't know about it until later, when Dad was determined I was going to leave school after Year 10, Miss Craig rang him up and told him that if it were a

matter of money, she would waive the fees. She gave me the chance to get the education I needed. She opened up the world for me. I found out later that she had died, and I hadn't had the opportunity to thank her.

Raimond Gaita described his early life in the memoir *Romulus, My Father*. He is one of Australia's most distinguished philosophers, unrivalled in his ability to bring classical moral concerns into contemporary debates. Given the austere humanity that characterises Raimond's writing, we were interested to notice his description of Martin Winkler, one of the teachers who changed his life.

Martin Winkler was perhaps the wisest man I have known. Eccentric, and a strong, passionate personality, he was more than a little daunting, but in Year 11 we became close because, threatened with expulsion from my school, I found refuge each week in his study [where I went for German lessons].

My most vivid memories of my school years—and the ones that still give me most pleasure and inspire my deepest gratitude—are of the times when Winkler went to the little organ he kept in his book-lined study and played Bach cantatas and talked about them to me. I was entranced by his untroubled confidence that he had revealed to me some of the great treasures of Western civilisation. It never occurred to me to ask why he did it because I knew, as everyone knows, that people enjoy sharing what they love. ...

For many years after I left school I visited Winkler at his home in Ballarat, and for many years he showed me love's role in teaching. With no pedagogical strategy about how to bridge my delinquent interests and ambitions and the fine things he put in my way, he never talked down to me. The quality of his attention to the things he loved made me trust their value and to trust in him.

Our third story comes from Nick Jose, writer, critic and Professor of Creative Writing. Nick sees himself as teaching what he was taught.

I learned to read literature from Mr Schubert. Although my practice has changed, that chord is still there. I think I'm incredibly lucky to have had such a good teacher. He was quite an imposing figure, partly because he was such a senior teacher, partly because he had the English and the German; that was another layer of learning. He also had a very distinctive croaky voice—we called him Frog Schubert—and a very big nose. He was almost a Gothic figure; one had a lot of respect for him, combined with a certain fear. He was quite a tough teacher, but very, very good.

Mr Schubert had a really deep love of literature. The texts he chose for us were fantastic texts he had a passion for, and, however strange his manner, he was able to convey that passion. He was very sensitive to literature and was always challenging us boys to be responsive as well. He was challenging us to tap into quite powerful forces in our lives, and that was a way of letting us be ourselves.

He seemed blissfully unaware of the effect he was having on us. He would be there, he would rub his nose a lot and he'd read out these bits, like the quote from *Othello*—'an old black ram … tupping your white ewe'. It was electrifying! Because he was blissfully unaware, we thought it was okay too. He treated us absolutely as if we were mature people intellectually. There was no talking down, and so that does lead to a kind of mutual respect.

Teaching in the Dark

All these accounts confirm that teaching is a discovery of new worlds. However mundane it is, with its chalkdust and its battle-scarred classroom furniture, with its idiosyncratic and life-worn teachers, teaching is also a matter of inspiration, revelation, awe, passion, intercession. Miss Craig, Martin Winkler and Mr Schubert were not just pouring their knowledge into students. They were teaching students how to live wisely. Instruction becomes an education when students learn about their lives.

The miracle of teaching, however, is often misunderstood by students. They sometimes imagine, as Betty Churcher did of Miss Craig, that their teachers have a God-like control of the process. But this is not how teachers experience the classroom. Although they are in awe of the profound significance of the process of education, teachers know that they are not in control of the most important things that happen in class. They experience the process through humility rather than omnipotence.

Raimond Gaita alludes to the teacher's humility when noting Martin Winkler's refusal to anticipate pedagogic outcomes. Nick Jose's teacher, Mr Schubert, made a similar demurral in his reply to a letter from a grateful student. Teaching, Mr Schubert insisted, was work that takes place in the dark:

> How thoughtful of you to guess what a letter like yours, coming out of the blue as it did, would mean to a teacher like me. A teacher's work can properly be judged only by its long-term outcome, of which, in the nature of things,

he can normally expect to know little or nothing: he works, as it were, largely in the dark.

Additionally, there is the question of what criterion it is appropriate to use. Recently, at a dinner at the School, I sat between [A], who was still plainly excited by being newly appointed a judge of the Supreme Court, and [B], who makes no bones about his satisfaction with his role in shaping the policies of the Reserve Bank. But, perversely perhaps, I am even more impressed by [C], who tells me he still always has his Donne on his bedside table, or [D], who claims that he reads more poetry than anything else.

Mr Schubert's teaching was based, presumably, on a range of hopes for his students. He hoped they would be successful in their careers; he hoped they would serve others; he hoped they would be sustained by their relationships with books. Doubtless his teaching had such outcomes. The paradox is that to achieve these outcomes, Mr Schubert set them aside in his daily classroom work. Like Martin Winkler, he concentrated on the students as they were, then and there. His task as teacher was to establish a classroom situation in which students' lives could be changed through their relation with John Donne. He didn't try to control the outcome of this relation. He just loved what he did, and he shared what he loved, and he had faith in his students and his beloved poets. As Nick Jose put it, speaking of Mr Schubert, 'What the teacher does is in the here and now, that's where it happens, and then there is this distant harvest, which they have to just trust in. Teachers can't predict exactly what will happen. Their work is an act of faith'.

The Greek philosopher Socrates, often described as the greatest pedagogue, characterised teaching as an impossible project. An awareness of this impossibility underlies Mr Schubert's bemusement about his effect on students. It was a bemusement shared by the teachers we interviewed. They were uneasy about our book's title, not thinking of themselves in heroic terms. As they told us, it is *teaching* that is powerful, not *teachers*; the miracle comes from what teachers and students do together. Teachers who try to change students are imposing themselves on students, thus limiting students to what the teachers can themselves imagine. Ethical teaching, they insisted, is about opening up students, ensuring they do their best at *whatever* they do. Because education is fundamentally a process of educing—drawing out—students must find their own ways. Teachers can accompany them but not do the learning or the living on their behalf.

In their different ways, our teachers were echoing the pedagogy espoused by the nineteenth-century essayist Ralph Waldo Emerson:

> The secret of Education lies in respecting the pupil. It is not for you to choose what he shall know, what he shall do. It is chosen and foreordained, and he only holds the key to his own secret. By your tampering and thwarting and too much governing he may be hindered from his end and kept out of his own. Respect the child. Wait and see the new product of nature.

The problem raised by teachers about our book's title is a real one, but not one that can be solved. The mystery of the teaching relationship, of *all* relationships, is that things happen that cannot be explained in terms of the finite individuals involved. Teaching and learning happens *between* and *through* students and teachers, without clearly identifiable sources.

TRUST IN THE CLASSROOM

Students, parents and education ministers probably all hope that today's schoolchildren will emerge with grateful stories like those of Helen, Betty, Raimond and Nick. But these stories challenge common assumptions about the relation between pedagogic strategy and success. The relation between a teacher and a student is as particular as that between two friends or between the members of a family. Its overall success comes as a by-product of the primary trust and attention that those in the relationship offer to each other. Certainly, as Mr Schubert tells us, the meaning of success will change as people are transformed by the relationship.

Stories of life-changing teachers show us that, at the heart of education, there is a tension between the desire for certainty and the need for trust and openness. On the one hand, people want teaching to predictably supply students with good values, with skills and knowledge, with good jobs. On the other hand, because it is based on learning, education is always orientated to openness. It is necessarily unsettling, especially to parents, who see their children change as education allows them to find their way. Many of the debates in education are beyond resolution because they are based, without acknowledgement, on this existential dilemma. There is no way to bring stability to a system that needs openness.

In every class, good teachers hold this tension between the desire for certainty and the need for openness. If, as a polity and civil society, we truly value education, we need to develop the same maturity: we need to realise that our anxious demands, and the policies they generate, may actually reduce educational opportunities, by interfering with the direct relation between teachers and students. Our schools are full of good teachers passionate about what they do. It is our responsibility to understand and encourage such teaching. When the awesome responsibility of teaching is recognised, teachers will be given the respect and trust they need to get on with their life-changing work.

———

Dawn Casey: Your Very Nature

Dawn Casey is known for her distinguished career in the public service, and, particularly, for her work as the first Director of the National Museum of Australia. She has a gift for managing large and complex organisations. Dawn told us that, as an Aboriginal student, she had experienced discrimination in schools, but there were also exceptional teachers who saw and encouraged her potential.

Looking back at primary school, there were a couple of really good teachers that I admired and responded to. I was a good student in terms of study, I tried really hard and I was an excellent sportsperson. There were issues on the other side in terms of being so poor, from an Aboriginal background, and with my parents knowing nothing about education. Being so poor you didn't have everything you needed so you felt a bit excluded. Now, looking back, it is interesting how you can see the very nature of what you are and what you will become. For example, I remember in Grade 3 directing a play. It was just amazing when you think about it. I had no books at home, but every now and then I would take library books home. I loved reading but I would get into trouble at home for reading because my mother was convinced that books make you lazy. So I used to read by moonlight. Anyway I remember being fascinated [by] *Beauty and the Beast*, so I said we should do it as the Christmas play, and I directed it. The teacher at that stage, I think her name was Mrs Hill, she encouraged us even though there was no drama in the school curriculum. So it was interesting. I think it happened because I'm a bit bossy and if I get an idea I just do it. I know what I am now, but what I remember is that we were allowed to do it and encouraged to do it by this teacher. So she was very good.

———

CHAPTER TWO

SEEING POTENTIAL IN STUDENTS

POTENTIAL

If sent from the classroom as punishment, Betty Churcher most feared being seen by Miss Craig, the headmistress. At the time, Betty probably imagined that Miss Craig would see her faults alone: remembering her 'crimes and misdemeanours', and her good but 'not brilliant' academic results, Betty thinks she must have been 'a bit of a thorn in Miss Craig's side'. But if Miss Craig saw the misdemeanours, she didn't respond to them in isolation. According to Betty, Miss Craig's greatness as a teacher came from her 'gift of being able to *see* her students, each one of them'.

> The interesting thing about Miss Craig was that she had spotted already, like God does, that I was on a path that would lead me towards art. I think she saw in me a seriousness, a passion. I used to skip ordinary classes, and stay down in the art room: now that would have been a cardinal sin, but she would turn a blind eye, which was extraordinary. She did everything she could to allow the art stream in me to flow. And she must have been doing that for every student.

The teacher's insight comes from their ability to see students as whole people. This point was emphasised by Jenny Oliver, a primary school teacher, when describing her maths teacher, Mr Simpson. In her senior high-school years, Jenny had become burdened by her own and other people's expectations. She had pigeonholed herself as a future lawyer or doctor on the basis of high marks. Rather than conform, she was on the point of dropping out entirely. Mr Simpson not only allowed her to find her way back, he helped her find her own vocation as a primary school teacher.

> He was so *there* for me, so gentle and so kind, and he listened to what I said when other teachers had lost their patience or didn't know what to do with me. Absolutely encouraging. When I think about teachers like him, I remember thinking: *They make me feel like me!* Mr Simpson got the picture, he got the whole personality. And I guess I became even more me because I was totally devoid of anxiety. When people have expectations of you they see one slice only, whereas Mr Simpson saw the whole and I could flourish.

Jenny was debilitated and constrained by the pressure of expectations; Mr Simpson made a difference because he saw that she would always be more than dux of her class, a doctor or a teacher, even if she were any of these things. By focusing on Jenny, and not on definitions of her, Mr Simpson helped her to relax and be herself, to find joyful ways of realising her potential. The world was again full of open promise.

When Miss Craig and Mr Simpson *saw* their students, they saw the potential that made each unique and incomparable. This insight is the essential attribute of teachers who change lives, for it underlies their ability to draw out the students' potential by drawing out the best work they can do. As Betty said of Miss Craig, the magical ability of teachers is to expect the best of their students no matter what they do in life.

While the ability to draw out potential is at the heart of good teaching, there are different understandings of the term with quite different implications for teaching. Potential is sometimes confused with talent, seen as a measure of innate ability. To see the student's potential in this sense is to assay them as raw material and, on the basis of this, set educational expectations. Jenny, for example, felt pressured to always excel, and expected herself to maintain her academic record. Although often presented as a form of praise, expectations based on the attribution of talent actually constrain the student's potential, establishing an identity that becomes a measure of their life. In the face of these expectations, Jenny experienced such anxiety that she lost a sense of the inherent value of education.

A richer sense of potential arises when teachers like Mr Simpson and Miss Craig see students in their uniqueness, as whole people whose capacities exceed any definition. Instead of setting up external standards that distract students from their current situations, these teachers only ask for what the students can do at any given moment—their best. All they require is that students commit themselves, refusing to hold back because they think they've done enough or reached their limit. They're asking not that students be the best but that they do their best.

Whereas talent is an objective thing that can be tested and measured from the outside, no words can describe potential. It comes as epiphany, Jenny told us: potential is not some *thing* that is seen but a sense of wonder that is experienced. The teacher can see the students' potential because students reopen the teacher's horizons:

What I see in the children in my class is their potential. It is an epiphany. For me as a teacher, it's an absolute privilege. When I look at them, when I look at their writing, and I see what they have the ability to be, oh my gosh, leaps and bounds beyond me! When I think about what I want them to learn, I want them to see what their potential is, and to realise it as best they can for themselves.

THE WHOLE PERSON

To spell out the difference between these forms of potential we'll consider the story of Diana Doherty, who is an international soloist and Principal Oboe with the Sydney Symphony Orchestra. At the age of twenty, Diana decided that her recognised talent could be perfected under the tutelage of a famous overseas oboist. 'I was very attracted to this teacher because he seemed to know everything, and I believed at that point that it was possible to have all the technical answers.' This teacher provided Diana with what she thought she wanted, teaching her how to sit, how to hold the oboe, how to breathe correctly, and so on, but Diana gradually became frustrated with the classes. With her particular physique, for example, she could not breathe well when she tried to fit the perfect model: the lessons were not addressing *her*, as she was, but requiring her to be something she couldn't be. What she needed was help in becoming the best that *she* could be. Diana summed up the experience by saying, 'I recall feeling *I just want him to appreciate me as a person, not just for the fact that I have talent; I want to feel valued as a whole*'.

Diana had been initially attracted to this teaching process by her identity as a student of potential: in trying to perfect her technique, she was trying to match a proffered expectation. But to reclaim her true potential she had to relinquish perfection.

To try and face up to perfection has been one of my personal issues, I guess, particularly when you've been told you have a lot of potential. So if I touch my instrument, I have to be brilliant otherwise I can't bear to. I'm expected to be good but I don't feel I can live up to that, so even just picking up an oboe alone in the room was very difficult. Apparently I've got potential but I seem to be my own worst enemy.

When Diana described herself as her own worst enemy, she was alluding to the relational structure established by expectations. She had become a critic in her own life, and had lost the ability to surprise or enjoy herself. As Diana put it, you have to care about excellence if you are to succeed, 'but being a perfectionist can also paralyse you; it can make life very difficult and can make progress difficult too'.

The issue of perfectionism came to a head in a series of international competitions. Like all perfectionists, Diana had a tendency to procrastinate, thereby providing herself with the alibi of under-preparedness if she was ever less than brilliant. Going into these competitions under-prepared for the later rounds, Diana emerged with disappointing results. The lessons were terrifyingly clear: her unrealistic fantasies were distracting her from what she loved; her perfectionism was a self-sabotage that prevented her responding to opportunities and giving them her best.

When Diana finally talked honestly with a friend about her struggle with expectations, she found that her demons released their hold on her. This was, she said, a 'moment of awareness that unlocked my potential': she could reconnect with her instrument and practise with enjoyment. Diana found she was playing the oboe with renewed interest, without assessing her performance against an external standard. The irony is, of course, that she won the next competition and found her career launched. The judges had clearly been able to hear something different in her playing. By altering her expectations of herself, Diana had changed her relation to the oboe and released the music.

As a teacher herself, Diana says that she can hear this difference, as a quality of heart. She says students 'who live and breathe music can play in a way that is almost like a bucket of water in the face':

> Somebody might play with technical proficiency but not have emotional engagement in what they are doing and it leaves you cold. Playing from the heart makes you connect with the audience. That's what really takes people along with you. At the same time it makes you very vulnerable: you kind of open your heart; I close my eyes and move to the music. You're vulnerable because somebody might look at you and think *Gosh you look stupid when you play*. You feel vulnerable because you're letting yourself go.

Whereas expectation is prediction, Diana refers to potential as surprise, openness and vulnerability. It is not definable, and cannot be prescribed, but it can be witnessed, experienced as an epiphany.

Diana's approach to teaching others has been shaped by her experience as a student. She has learned to teach with the unique difference of each student rather than seeking to produce the perfect oboist. 'Some teachers in certain insecure situations want to establish their authority by being critical, but if somebody rings me up and says, *Can I have a lesson?*, I say, *No, but come along and we'll work together*, because I see it as an opportunity.' She describes this relational teaching as wholistic. It involves 'just looking out for this individual person, at their body, at the way their mind works, at the way they talk to themselves'. She is not just teaching oboe;

she is helping students develop ways of dealing with themselves: 'how to encourage themselves, how to analyse themselves without putting themselves down. To put it simply, it's teaching them how to grow through this example of looking at one thing, the oboe, specifically.'

In the light of Diana's story, we can better understand Miss Craig's expectations. When she expected *the best* of her girls, she was not presuming to judge or compare them, for each was unique. She had faith that if the girls went about their lives with an open heart, they would find their unique paths and fulfil their potential. What she expected was that they would maintain openness, an honest relation with their lives. Her job was to help them develop awareness of issues that might alienate them from their work, and she did this by drawing their attention to occasions when their work was anything less than wholehearted.

Betty remembers Miss Craig conveying the sense 'that being at school was a serious business, and that whatever you did in life, you took it seriously'. Miss Craig herself applied this rule by taking each girl seriously; in doing so she challenged them to ask whether they were taking their own lives as seriously. Through this challenge she taught them that excellence doesn't arise from a desire for your own perfection; it comes from a devotion to what you are doing. A sense of wholeness comes not from reaching a peak, but from the wonder of learning how to do more.

A WHOLE NEW WORLD

A wholistic approach is often misunderstood as a process of summing all aspects of a person (intellectual factors, plus emotional factors, plus physical factors, plus …). The person, according to this model, is an identity who can be known completely. True wholism, on the other hand, is relational, based on a principle of infinite connection. When Diana is playing oboe, for example, it is the connection with the audience that allows her potential to be given form. She is whole, playing from the heart, when she is open and vulnerable, without a sense of finite borders.

If education, then, is a process of realising the whole that is potential, the teacher's role is to offer new connections and contexts. Facts dispensed in lessons are always more than increments to the student's store of knowledge; they are connections that change the meaning of what's known and of what can be known. They are connections that allow students to expand by simultaneously giving them a sense of a new and enlarged world.

Teachers used the word 'experience' to describe this connecting knowledge. Their job, they told us, was to bring their experience to the classroom, enlivening the dry knowledge of textbooks by showing its relevance, by putting it into context. High-school teacher Judith Moreland-Mitchell said,

> I've read; I've studied; I've travelled; I've had many life experiences; I'm interested in many things. So I can interconnect all these subjects for students. Everything just falls into place—you open up a whole world to them.

When Judith says that she can *interconnect subjects* for her students, she implies that teachers offer themselves as a bridge between worlds. Teachers must know what they know and must simultaneously imagine the world from the child's perspective. As the connections they offer come to life for students, the teacher disappears: students have learned a subject when the connections have become their own. As philosopher Michel Serres says, '[a]s a living interchanger, the guide or pedagogue has a double body: one which is capable of addressing childhood and another which leads childhood towards a world in which, so far from walking, one flies' (1995: 166).

For Betty Churcher, this new world first appeared when, as an eight year old, she suddenly connected with the picture *Evicted* in the National Gallery of Queensland. She saw an autumn day in Cornwall, a family being evicted from its home. Around the family lay leaves that looked so crackly Betty wanted to reach out and scoop them up.

> This little girl being evicted was looking straight out at me, she was about my age, and I thought if I should ever be able to paint like that, wow. And I think that was probably the beginning of it. I felt absolute wonder that you could create a world, a complete little self-contained world that could sit in the Queensland Gallery. It was just that ability to recreate another environment, another whole world, another whole set of people with their own stories. And that was the magic of creation.

Betty's *wow* was a revelatory moment in which she saw the potential of art. Standing in front of a picture, her place in the world changed utterly: she was no longer simply in Brisbane; she was standing in the tradition of Western art; she was in a street in Cornwall; she was in an English artist's studio. She was no longer simply herself. 'Yes, another world, another place, another time, the magic carpet has just transported you and *pop*, there you are, not in Brisbane any more, in 1939, but you are in Cornwall in England, in Victorian times.' Having seen *Evicted*, Betty knew that anyone who told her she was only in Brisbane was locking her out of a bigger world to which she belonged.

If art was one magic carpet, Betty's school was another. The distance from home to school could not be measured in kilometres because Somerville House expanded her horizons and unleashed her imagination. Betty described her life before Somerville House in terms of 'certain prescribed roles':

If I was told once it was inappropriate because I was a girl, I was told a thousand times. Mum had certain very strict rules about what my brother could do and what I couldn't do, and I found that terribly frustrating, because I wanted to be independent, to be out there, to be able to do things, to go down to the creek and play, or go into town. None of those things were allowed me.

When Betty arrived at Somerville House she felt liberated. Here was a diverse group of students, with different interests and abilities, not being constrained by their sex. Her school friends gave her glimpses of her own potential: in seeing what other students could do, she learnt what she might do too. 'Because it was an all-girls school it gave me that freedom of movement. We were all able to do the same things, there weren't levels or strata of behaviour.'

The teachers also provided Betty with role models:

Pat Prentice arrived on the scene when I was in Year 9 and she was a person with a genuine passion. *There's a world out there*, she'd say, *go get it*. She might go to Melbourne and she would come back bubbling with enthusiasm; she'd been to the ballet and she'd come back so enthusiastic that all I wanted to do was get to Melbourne and go to the ballet. So it was that sort of infectious enthusiasm. I remember her once saying to me, *You can either be a big fish in a little pond, or you can be a little fish in a big pond. Which do you want?* And I said, *Well I think I'd like to be a big fish*, and she said, *Very boring moving in a little pond*, and I said, *Then I'll be the little fish in the big pond*, and that was the sort of world that she gave me. I could stay in Brisbane all my life and be a celebrity or give up the idea of celebrity and enjoy what's out there.

Betty said that Pat Prentice gave her a sense that 'maybe I could do something, and perhaps go overseas and spread my wings a bit'. There's an interesting paradox here, in the mixed metaphor of little fish and outstretched wings. Whereas a big fish lives in fear of competition that might deprive it of its distinction, a little fish feels expanded by the challenges of the world. Competition for the latter is not about proving that you are the best, but finding out what you can do and what part you can play. Whereas the big fish has an insatiable desire for self-confirmation, the small fish is moved by curiosity and possibility. It feels both humbled and enlarged by being part of something limitless. This is the combination of humility and wonder that allows people to feel whole.

After leaving school, Betty applied for a scholarship to the Royal College of Art in London.

> I felt *I've got to test myself against something bigger than Brisbane*. And I won the scholarship, which was brilliant, and that was the best thing that's ever happened to me in my life. It was all my dreams come true. Nothing else ever touched it. I thought *I'm out of here. I'm going to have a whole new life!* It was just such bliss to be away from home.

Having tested herself in London, Betty could return to Australia and see it, not as a place of exile, but as part of a bigger world. She could experience the whole world through the particularities of being an Australian woman, an artist, an art gallery director, a mother.

A DIVERSE COMMUNITY

Betty's particular passion was art, but her school friends would have had different aptitudes. The important thing about a school that opens worlds is that it encourages and connects these diverse interests. Through an effervescent sense of community, students share each other's passions.

One of the many interviewees who stressed the importance of the full life of a school was radio broadcaster Julie McCrossin. Although the girls at Julie's school 'worked terribly hard and competed ferociously' in academic areas, exam preparation was only one part of the life of the school.

> High school was about getting into as many university faculties as you could, but that was just part of the school. It was also about the house plays, the debating, excursions to museums and universities. There was a lot of emphasis on learning for its own sake. There was even a sense that that was the better learning.
>
> The performing arts assist language acquisition and learning; sporting activity in younger children assists the development of literary skills. There's plenty of research that supports what was happening at SCEGGS [Sydney Church of England Girls' Grammar School]. It was and still is a powerhouse of activity.
>
> I was active in the choir; I had to do my homework frantically so I could take part in full-scale productions of the *Messiah*. Now I look back and realise that it was enriching my capacity to learn and was informing my essays. It wasn't irrelevant to the HSC, but it wasn't directly relevant either.

Julie's school offered diversity in both curricular and extra-curricular activities. When a school is a *powerhouse of activity*, this diversity doesn't fragment the community or produce narrowly specialised students. On the contrary, the potential of each student is drawn out by connections between students, between activities, and between the school and the broader community.

A performance of the *Messiah*, for example, will bring families and friends into the school and take students beyond the school; it will develop students' ability to work with each other in choirs and orchestras; it will bring to life for students the form, aesthetic and historical context of eighteenth-century music.

The breadth of this education offered Julie a sense of values that has stayed with her. Learning the value of openness, students don't become narrow or inflexible, focused on only one activity. Learning to value the process of learning itself, they are too passionate to be instrumental about the lives they are leading.

The richness and diversity in school culture is, we found, a decisive factor for many parents selecting schools for their children. As a parent told us,

> I want the education you'd expect plus other things we cannot give at home, like extra languages and music. I want the school to foster different sorts of talents without knowing what these talents might be. It should be a creative environment, with lots of different ideas that will stimulate different aspects in the children.

Extracurricular activity, however, is not just seen as a bonus or as a way to extra accomplishments; it is valued as a sign that students are being respected as fully rounded people. Encouraging extra interests is regarded as a basic requirement of a good education. Another parent said,

> We chose our daughter's school after years of agonising and looking at countless schools. Academically, socially, it's very diverse: it's got a very nice culture there. The values are those of cultural inclusiveness and respect. And they really encourage the girls to get involved in all sorts of things. They have lots of opportunities. There's music and

drama, for example, and they have a Shakespeare festival that the kids really love. There's no limit to the involvement except that the school has high expectations academically. The headmistress says that the school provides all the activities; it's up to the parents and the students to manage the time.

A diverse school offers everyone the chance to excel at something; it also offers everyone the precious opportunity to be valued when they are *not* the best. Students learn that there are some activities at which they fail, and others which they enjoy without honours. They learn that achievements are important but are only part of life. They learn openness to different experiences, and respect for difference. They learn the value of cooperation, and the difference between creative and destructive competition.

The diversity of activities and aptitudes are gathered in school assemblies. Students and teachers, and even parents, are there to celebrate the life of the school, to share in each other's successes and failures and efforts. In a *powerhouse of activity*, *ferocious competition* is transformed into an inclusive spirit of cooperation. A school's culture is rich when applause for each person is recognition for the role of every person. The school is teaching values by valuing everyone's unique contribution. As a parent told us, this is a matter of soul, of values:

A sense of community is very important. It is soulless to go somewhere where you are not part of something bigger. I went to a new government school but it had a sense of community that you could feel. There was a sense of excitement, of something happening. Someone was doing brilliantly in music or maths, or someone had won a literary prize, or we had a great football team. It was important and good and I knew I was lucky to be there.

INTERCESSION

If the role of education is to broaden the child's horizons, students will be continually changing in unforeseen ways. It is easy for both parents and teachers to lose touch with these changes by holding on to certain expectations. Parents and teachers have a responsibility to help each other remain open.

Betty Churcher's father, for example, had wanted her to leave school after Year 10, fearing that further education would only raise false hopes, but Miss Craig persuaded him to allow Betty to continue at school. With her wide experience in the education of girls, she could see Betty's life in a broader context than her father could. She had seen women take up many occupations, and she'd seen the spark in Betty. Her role as a teacher was to intercede on behalf of Betty's potential.

This story highlights the complementarity of parent and teacher. Each needs the other if, together, they are to do the work of raising children; each reminds the other that no one knows everything about the child and that no one can abrogate the child's life. In this joint work of child-rearing, one of the teacher's contributions is to see the child anew, in a different context. Elizabeth Game talked of this when comparing her roles as parent and as high-school teacher:

> Teachers give students someone they can surprise, someone who has an open mind about them. The distance in their relationship can allow teachers to see students' potential without being blinded by too many expectations. They give the child the chance to be seen outside the familiar family context: the child can feel valued because they are not seen in comparison with their siblings, or in terms of the domestic balance or imbalance, or in the context of the parents' occupations or directions.

So that when the teacher says to the child *You were very good at that triple jump*, and the child comes from the family that has no athletic sense of pride, that's a huge new experience for that child.

Teachers, Elizabeth says, help parents overcome their preconceptions. Because parents are so close to their children, they can be fearful of letting them go, afraid of what life can and indeed will do to them. In such states, parents see projections of their own fantasies and fears, but do not see their children. Putting this uncharitably, Ralph Waldo Emerson spoke of the 'self-love in the parent [that] desires that his child should repeat his character and fortune'. As Emerson implies, this is an expectation which the good teacher will help the child 'nobly disappoint'. In doing so, the teacher will also help the parent, for by speaking on behalf of the parent's better inclinations, they allow them to reconnect with their child through a truer love.

Vilma Rotellini, a primary school teacher, gave an example of the teacher's role in nobly disappointing the expectations of parents:

The parents see the kids one way at home, but we see them differently. It could be reading, and the child is masking it very well, even to the parents. They think their child is really coping with everything, is very bright, and they're really in denial that their child has got some concerns with reading. I would never lie to a parent. I would gently but firmly make them aware of what I see, suggest we get some testing done, and maybe look back at things that happened in other years that they haven't recognised or admitted. So sometimes there is a problem of parents in denial.

The teacher's clarity comes from the most poignant aspect of their vocation: they know they must let go their students at the end of the year. Telling us how heartbreaking this parting could be, teachers nonetheless acknowledged that it was necessary to fulfilling their responsibilities. As kindergarten teacher Vicky Yannakouros said, 'the end of the year is tinged with sadness, but it's also a nice feeling; we've got through a year successfully and it's time to move on and that's all part of the growing process'. More clearly than parents sometimes, teachers know that they cannot control children's lives; they must simply do the best they can for the time that they are with them. The letting go allows teachers to see students as they are; they can intercede honestly because they are not vainly trying to protect students from life itself.

If the teacher's role is to speak on behalf of the student's potential, teachers can, at times, become biased about students. When this happens they rely on the intercession of parents: the space between teachers and parents safeguards the potential of students. A parent described having to intercede when her child was accused of stealing a calculator:

He was under a cloud and I thought he was innocent. At this school these incidents are handled in a democratic manner, but the teacher and principal are of course much more skilled than students in handling these meetings. As a parent it is difficult to judge when the student has gone as far as they can in representing themselves. In this case it seemed to me that the Common Law presumption of innocence wasn't operating. They had a crime and were saying *Well, unless you can explain where the calculator is, you must have done it.*

In preventing the teachers from unjustly judging her child, this parent was helping the school maintain the trusting relation upon which education relies.

Teachers also rely on the intercession of other teachers. At the end of the year, teachers don't just hand students back to parents, they hand them on to the next teacher. The responsibilities shared between parent and teacher are mirrored in the responsibilities shared between teachers at a school. Students need a variety of teachers to ensure that no one teacher becomes a model to be followed. Students are encouraged to find their own way as different teachers draw out different aspects of their potential. It takes a whole school community to educate a child.

CULTIVATING POTENTIAL

Many of our interviewees spoke of potential through metaphors of organic growth. The writer Drusilla Modjeska spoke of her teacher Miss Vallance 'planting a seed', Jenny Oliver said that Mr Simpson let her 'flourish', Judith Moreland-Mitchell spoke of students 'blossoming'. Raimond Gaita also evoked this image:

> Years after I first met [Martin Winkler], when I despaired of teaching, he told me that there are two ways to think about teaching. One is to dream of pulling a switch that will make a thousand lights come on. Another is nourished by the image of passing a candle from one person to another, or of planting seeds, not knowing when or where they will grow. It was the wisest advice about teaching that I have ever received. The seeds he planted in me were then still germinating. They grew only many years later, when I wrote *Good and Evil: An Absolute Conception*, which I dedicated to him.

Whereas the logic of prediction presupposes an already deter-mined world, a finite world without creative possibilities, potential is experienced in a living, organic world. To anyone with eyes to see, the seed has within it not only the history of life, but an evolutionary potential that is never finalised. Each seed is unique, yet each is the whole miracle of life. Good teaching relies on the ability to see this universal essence in the uniqueness of each student.

It is this logic of potential that accounts for the remarkable fact that teachers find qualities in a world governed by quantities. However many students they have in a year, however many years they have taught, good teachers find the unlimited capacity to be amazed by the uniqueness of each student. Competition is used in schools to help students extend themselves, but teachers' relations to students aren't based on competitive rankings. There is no com-petition for the teacher's respect.

When we asked Sharon Cheers, a primary school teacher, what she saw in her students, she spoke of their blooming. She saw in each their particularity:

> You can definitely see talent in people, but you can also see them as a person. That constantly amazes me. You can go down to that preschool and their personalities are there. They are true little people. So in saying you can see their talent, you can certainly see aspects of their person-ality that are strong, but whether or not that's a talent or just them, I don't know. In terms of something that you measure, in terms of competition, I wonder: *Competition in what? Competition in being a good person? Competition in being able to answer closed questions correctly? How do you measure a good thinker against a better thinker?* You can always set some-thing you can measure and then compare students against

that, but that's leaving out a whole lot. I suppose that's the whole other thing, how do you measure education?

An aspect of the teacher's nurturing role, Sharon insisted, was the ability to accommodate the different potentials of each student. She gave an example:

I remember a boy who rolled on the floor for half of Year 1. And you would think *Gosh, what is going on in this boy's head?* He was just the most amazing thinker and said the most amazing things, but just could not sit at a desk, or do any of those things. In the end that really didn't matter; well, it mattered that he couldn't conform to school expectations, but it didn't mean that he wasn't learning, and I could be flexible, so it was OK. But I thought he had an amazing mind. And that's that thing about knowing kids. If you know them, you can nurture that strength and get that response. And that doesn't mean that it's the same way you get to another child, or that another child is the same. If you see them as a little person, not as something that we're trying to mould into something else, then you just work with what you've got. I think that requires an openness.

Sharon is a passionate teacher, but her devotion requires her to live with uncertainty. Like Martin Winkler's, her tone has hope but no triumphalism. She knows that any attempt to guarantee the outcomes of teaching removes the life of the process. We can plant seeds, and cultivate the vulnerable seedlings in our care, but their fate is as open to delight and disappointment as the rest of life. We cannot control life but if we can learn from its ups and downs, we can grow, and it is growth that gives life a sense of wholeness.

Leslie Devereaux:
Education as Unfolding

Having worked as an anthropologist at university, Leslie Devereaux is now a psychotherapist who is involved in the training of therapists. We spoke to Leslie because of her special interest in the supportive environment that is essential to good parenting, teaching and therapy. It is this environment that allows for the unfolding of potential.

Fear is the greatest impingement on the capacity to learn, because it stops us being able to think. We can see it quite clearly in children: a chaotic and frightening environment inhibits the unfolding of the child's curiosity. If relational therapy is based on creating an environment in which we can re-start an unfolding process which has been traumatically impinged upon, then by implication we're saying that good parenting has allowed something similar to go on most of the time. The degree to which parents can be their child's teacher or therapist depends on the extent to which a parent can refrain from defining the child. That's why we have training and supervision of therapists: we just have to be able to distinguish our own traumas and our own kind of reactive processes and know something about when we're in them.

There is a lovely idea in Zen about helping someone have that first enlightenment experience. The Zen student presents themselves to the teacher over and over again and the teacher is waiting until they begin to hear the chicken pecking inside the egg. At that point they watch very closely, because if the chicken can't quite break the membrane, it will die, but the chick will also die if the teacher breaks the membrane too soon. So that's the call and response of human existence: the teacher waits until the pecking is happening, and then only adds a little peck here and there, because it's the energy of the chicken that actually has to break the membrane.

Relatedness is a form of love. When I think of psychic intimacy, I think about it as the moments in which a person feels able to show delicate aspects of their inner life to another person and to feel that they won't be crushed and will be appreciated. Love, for me, in all these relationships has a mutual joy that comes when you are interested in a respectful way.

CHAPTER THREE

TEACHING AS A FORM OF LOVE

LOVE AND EDUCATION

The teacher's ability to see students as whole people comes from their relationship with students. Relationship gives teachers capacities to see and know what wouldn't otherwise be available. More particularly, it is the loving quality of the relationship that gives teachers enhanced understanding.

The word 'love' arose unselfconsciously in all our interviews, yet it is absent from public discussions of education. This silence reflects a severely diminished appreciation of both love and education. If we don't speak of love, we cannot understand why the greatest pedagogues in all cultures—from Socrates to Confucius, from Jesus to Buddha—have insisted that an education without love is an education without depth or life. The connection between learning and love is embedded in the very word 'philosophy' (*philo*: love; *sophia*: wisdom). It is a connection, primary school teacher Vicky Yannakouros told us, that underlies her work as a teacher:

> What do primary teachers do? I know this is going to sound simple, but first of all we love and care for people's

children. That really struck me a couple of years ago. I received a card from a kindy parent, who just wrote *Thanks for loving my child*. That was the only message. To know that your child is truly loved and cared for in that whole sense must be for a parent the most reassuring thing. And then obviously the education beyond that. As clichéd as that sounds, we need to love and care for children.

A teacher, Vicky went on to say, works through a love for the students, a love of teaching and a love of learning. What, we want to know, is the nature of this love? How does it differ from other forms of love?

RESPECT AND CLASSROOM ETHICS

We have distinguished two ways in which students can be seen, either as entities with definable talents, or as unique beings for whom no definition is adequate. These two ways of seeing arise from two ethical forms, which the philosopher Martin Buber spoke of as I–It and I–Thou. By helping us understand the different ethical situations that arise in teaching, Buber's terms will allow us to appreciate the role of love, respect and care in education.

The hyphenated form of I–It and I–Thou indicates that the I is not a fixed identity. In different forms of relation, we are different people, with different capacities. The I of I–It is a subject who, in aspiring to stand alone, surveys the world in terms of his or her own position and desires. The world becomes an array of objects, a set of means to the subject's ends. Whenever the world challenges the subject's knowledge, the surprise is taken as a threat to this position. The acquisition of knowledge is designed to maximise control by minimising surprise. It was this I–It relation that dominated Diana Doherty's life when she was seeking technical means to perfection as an oboist. Through her lessons and practice sessions, she sought control over the oboe.

Rather than standing alone, the I of the I–Thou relation is connected with others. In this relation, the world is not a set of external things but a whole that is always emerging through meetings. Think of the potential Diana finds when she *connects* with her audience, instrument and music. This is a situation where things happen relationally without arising from a subject's volition. The music emerges through Diana but is not self-consciously controlled by her. She no longer treats it as an object to be mastered. As Buber put it, 'The life of human beings is not passed in the sphere of transitive verbs alone. It does not exist in virtue of activities alone which have some *thing* for their object' (1958: 4).

Buber's point is that many of the most important relationships are unbounded, involving neither subjects nor objects:

> *It* exists only through being bounded by others. But when *Thou* is spoken, there is no thing. *Thou* has no bounds.
>
> When *Thou* is spoken, the speaker has no *thing*; he has indeed nothing. But he takes his stand in relation. ...
>
> The relation to the *Thou* is direct. No system of ideas, no foreknowledge, and no fancy intervene between *I* and *Thou*. (Buber, 1958: 4, 11)

When Buber says *the speaker has no thing*, he is referring to states of epiphany characterised by wonder. These are the states that allow teachers to *see* their students, and allow students to see the potential of their studies. When Vicky Yannakouros describes what she sees in her kindergarten students, she talks of this boundless no-thingness:

> The little children, they just look at you with this look of wonder about the world. They have these innocent faces, very open, and this incredible thirst for and love of learning. They want to hear what you've got to say. They think

it's really exciting. And then they want to tell you what they know about what you're talking about. It's beautiful. It's like they're hearing about something for the first time ever. It's when I realise this that I am blown away yet again by this incredible job that we have. It's quite goose-bumpy stuff.

The way in which these children and this teacher are present to each other exemplifies the directness of the I–Thou relation. They know each other's names, each other's faces; the teacher keeps meticulous files on the progress of each student. These are all necessary I–It forms of knowledge. But on this occasion, teacher and students see beyond these things to the undefended essence of each person. Without denying the objective truth of I–It claims, the I–Thou reveals that the whole person is more than this collection of attributes.

This revelation of the universal in a particular person is what Vicky means when she speaks of the beauty of open encounter. Beauty is not cuteness or attractiveness, or some *thing* you see, it is a way of seeing, of being and of knowing. Vicky has the creative eye of the portrait artist who sees the naked beauty in a particular face or gesture. She does not look *at* the children; instead, it is their bright eyes that allow her to see the potential they share.

Vicky's goose bumps arise from the wonder of such meeting. These children and this teacher, each so different, have come together, though they couldn't have imagined this a year before. Each happily places their life in the hands of others, who amaze them by allowing them to be really themselves. The goose bumps are awareness of the love and respect that allow the teacher and students to know each other's boundlessness directly, through a meeting with difference. Such a meeting, says Buber, is where life happens. Through this encounter we may develop objective knowledge about the other and yet, amazingly, this growing familiarity doesn't diminish the other's difference.

Clearly an instance of an I–Thou relation, the encounter in Vicky's classroom is based on a mutual respect for the vulnerability, openness and innocence of all participants. Clearly too this respect is not people simply affirming each other's identity. The respect of the I–Thou relation is, instead, awareness of Thou's unidentifiable essence, Thou's difference even to the way they identify themselves. Respect is always respect for this mystery. This is why it is not earned or forfeited. To carry out her teaching duties, Vicky must occasionally identify and rank children, in I–It mode, but it is the I–Thou that guides her, regularly reminding her of what teaching is really about. In this mode, Vicky could not treat children who have misbehaved with less respect than well-behaved ones, nor clever children with more respect than less gifted ones.

Vicky highlighted this point when she elaborated on the significance of the teacher's love:

> Love isn't about just thinking that the students are cute. It's the fact that I want my children to be validated as human beings and as individuals. I want my care and love of them to show to them that they have an important part in this huge, crazy world. Love is about respect and validation: that you matter enough for me to listen to you and accept what you've got to say and that you've got a contribution to make. It doesn't matter who you are. I want that bond to be real, so I need to be real with them. I need to show them also that respect is a two-way thing. I do respect them as people, as I hope they respect me.

When she *validates* students, Vicky accepts them just as they are, whole unique beings. They belong in this *huge, crazy world* because they make an incalculable difference in it. This is a form of respect that avoids the jealousy and competition that go with the finite logic of I–It. Because the I–Thou is boundless, respect for one child is not a threat to others: it is respect for all beings, acknowledgement of the different contribution that each makes.

Vicky's account of classroom ethics makes a crucial pedagogic point. The respect of the I–Thou relation is not only respect for other participants in the classroom, it is a respect for the surprises that must exist if there is to be learning. The I–Thou relation allows Vicky and her students to appreciate the amazing things they can learn from each other, and the amazing things they are still to learn about the world.

Whereas the I of I–It sees encounter as a frustrating loss of control, the I of I–Thou is grateful for the world that encounter opens. This is the world that makes us whole, that draws out our potential, that educates us. Only when wonder makes us aware of difference can we learn. We cannot learn, then, and we cannot know that there is more to learn, unless we learn with love and respect.

The role of love and respect in learning clarifies contemporary debates about the teaching of values. Politicians often claim that schools have become value-neutral and that lessons in values need to be reintroduced to the curriculum. All good teaching, however, is always based on the teaching of such values as respect for difference. Knowledge and ethics are inseparable. When teachers talk about values they are only reinforcing the deeper lessons learned through classroom relations.

A LOVE THAT ISN'T DESIRE

According to Buber, the I–Thou relation *is* love:

> Love is *between I* and *Thou* ... The man who does not know this, with his very being know this, does not know love ... Love ranges in its effect through the whole world.

> In a wonderful way, [through love] ... he can be effective,
> helping, healing, educating, raising up, saving. Love is
> responsibility of an *I* for a *Thou*. (1958: 14–15)

If love is the I–Thou, it is not, as is often assumed, confined
to or based upon familial or erotic situations. It is more funda-
mental than these. Moreover, love takes different forms in different contexts. The love of parents and children, for example,
complements the love of teachers and students, but they are not
the same.

Love, Buber insists, is misunderstood when it is seen as personal,
a feeling that one person has for another person, rather than relational, a way of being that arises between me and you. We are
fully implicated in love, but our involvement isn't personal because
love suspends the concerns of the ego on which personal identity
is based. Love isn't something we *do* but a state that we are in. It
follows that love isn't a source of subjective bias; instead, it removes
the personal attachments that produce dishonesty and distraction.
Love inclines us to truth and beauty.

As an I–Thou relation, love is based on respect rather than
desire. Buber's emphasis on the *between* in the I–Thou relation is
his way of insisting that love isn't a subject's desire for an object.
The infinitude of love and respect suspend the finite distinctions
between subjects and objects, lover and beloved. We found this
infinitude expressed in descriptions of the love of learning:

> I loved my teacher because he loved what I loved.

> I love you Miss K (a hand-drawn card, given to a kinder-
> garten teacher).

> I think she loved teaching, I think she loved the English
> language and I think she loved the girls, in a pure sense.

> You need to teach the love of learning itself.

You can only teach subjects you love, otherwise you just go through the motions.

I love teaching.

To teach well, you first of all have to love the children.

She loved maths with a passion and made me love it.

What I learned from her was the love. Her love for art was what was communicated.

My teacher was someone I loved and idolised. It was almost a crush at one stage. And she ignited that passion for drama that I didn't even realise I had.

I loved *Hamlet* and I loved Mrs MM.

I loved school; it was all about school.

I saw teachers who were passionately in love with what they were teaching.

She couldn't have taught me that parsing and analysis so thoroughly and so well if she hadn't loved it.

Taken together, these quotations do not take the I–It form: there is no defined object that is loved. Rather than loving just the teachers or just the subject or just the school, students experienced a love that connected teachers, students, subjects and school and which led on to a creative curiosity. This love held within it the love of the teachers, the love for the teachers, the love for the subject and the love of a life of learning. *I loved* Hamlet, *I loved Mrs MM*; *I loved my teacher because he loved what I loved*: there is no clear causality in such statements. Mrs MM is the doorway to *Hamlet*, but equally, *Hamlet* is the doorway to Mrs MM, and both doors open wonders beyond. Even in the case of the student who had the crush on her teacher, the teacher was not the end point of the love; the crush was a manifestation of her love for drama which was a manifestation of her own previously unrecognised potential. As one student put it, it's the love itself that is communicating and being communicated. The love that allows learning is, then, a love without end. Whereas desire brings learning to a halt by settling on an object, love reveals the possibilities of the world.

What happens if, by contrast, love settles on an object? When the lover defines themselves through the beloved person or thing, there is an I–It relation. The beloved is objectified, desired as an idealised reflection of the lover. This is an ethic that blocks learning because it disrespectfully denies difference. Without difference, the desirous self is closed off from the whole and potential is reduced to the narrowness of a subject's aims.

In the everyday classroom, this emerges as an issue of over-familiarity. Aware of the danger of identification, teachers told us of the importance of maintaining relationships based on respect rather than desire. The danger of desire is that it distracts both teachers and students from what's really going on. To keep people aware of the nature of the classroom relation, teachers need a certain im-personality and bearing, according to high-school physics teacher Kym Lawry:

> Teachers are in a privileged position with students and the potential to do harm is enormous. Of course, there are going to be students [who] idolise you and think you're fantastic. You need to make it clear in everything you do that you're not about building a close personal relationship with them. That's one of the most important things. It's to do with the extent that you divulge personal things about your life. Most often it's not appropriate.
>
> It's not about friendship or getting the students to like you: I mean you want them to like you and feel positively

towards you, but you must not focus on this. It's a very fine line. A lot of it is conveyed in your bearing; that sounds a bit pompous doesn't it? If I find students who speak to me in a way that shows they're not understanding our situation, it's my job as an adult to maintain the appropriate level in the relationship. Even if you do something that does push that student away a bit, even if it's slightly bruising, they just need to know *Hold on, that's not what we're on about.*

The problem of classroom favourites, which worries both students and parents, is an issue of overfamiliarity. It is often the case that teachers get on better with some students than others. The formality of the classroom ensures that this doesn't turn into favouritism, which would endanger all students by leaving them vulnerable to the teacher's personal likes.

Pastoral Care

Love and care go together, and teachers who see their students' potential cannot help but care for them. This care is not a supplement to the teacher's pedagogic responsibilities, but intrinsic to them, as high-school English teacher Barbara Devlin insisted: 'Pastoral care underpins everything we do as teachers. Making sure students are the best they can be in your subjects, and dealing with them as individuals—that is a pastoral care role'. A parent made the point even more explicitly when explaining how the rigour of a basic education only emerged through the care and carefulness of the teacher:

If you know children, you know their strengths and weaknesses. A perceptive teacher can identify signals and won't gloss over things. They will be aware of particular areas where children are nervous or lacking confidence, and they'll give them safe ways to develop these areas. Good teachers have sympathy, an ability to see beneath particular behaviours and intuit things. Not necessarily to know what is going on, but to know that something is going on, and then to have persistence and care and interest and a sense of responsibility to follow through on that. If a child isn't answering questions, it could mean several different things. It takes a sensitivity to make sure students don't fall through the academic net.

As this parent implies, teachers' care is not the same as that of parents, social workers or counsellors. Teachers who lose sight of the particularity of educational care will find their care compromised by an unhealthy desire to know and do everything for students. In Buber's terms, the teachers' responsibilities are 'for that realm of life allotted and entrusted to [them] for which [they] are able to respond' (1966: 19). The school and classroom are the centre of this allotted realm, though the teachers' care will spread through the students' lives.

We can learn much about a teacher's pastoral role from Jenny Oliver's description of Mr Simpson. Having been dux for many years, Jenny had become trapped by expectations; it was Mr Simpson who helped her through.

Mr Simpson was twofold, a great maths teacher and a constant for me. There was a period in Year 12 when I stopped going to school for a while and that caused trauma. One teacher phoned Mum and Dad, not knowing what to do, and some teachers made remarks about my failure to cope. But Mr Simpson never did that. I remember him taking me aside, and I said, *I don't want to be a lawyer or a doctor, I don't want to be a person cooped up in an office working 9 to 5. What do I need this school for? I'm just going to go and get a job.* He listened and said, *I understand where you are. I'm not like that either; I wouldn't like office work. Why do you think I'm a teacher?* He was gentle when other teachers had lost their patience.

Maybe as an adult he could understand; I actually respect him for probably understanding what was going on for me. I can see now that he was a father figure in some respects. I looked up to him, I respected him. It's interesting: I know girls who talked about having crushes on him, but it was not that for me. He was asexual, a leader, in a category of his own. It was based on that distance, the lack of familiarity, the respect that it bred. Whereas my relation with other adults at that stage was mixed up with trepidation, yucky emotion, with Mr Simpson it was calm, totally devoid of anxiety.

Especially interesting is Jenny's emphasis on Mr Simpson's teacherliness. His constancy of care was part of his excellence as a maths teacher, and characterised by a respect that ensured he didn't become identified with her problems. Mr Simpson knew something about what was going on in Jenny's life, and he was available if she needed to talk about her problems, but he didn't try to solve these problems. He kept his attention on educational relations, establishing a reliable classroom environment where Jenny could rediscover the love of learning. In this way, through *the lack of familiarity*, he gave her a breathing space.

Mr Simpson was *in a category of his own*, and it was this difference that gave Jenny opportunity to rediscover her own. When she surprised herself with the realisation that her life didn't entirely revolve around her anxieties, she could reconnect with her potential. Jenny had dropped out of school because she couldn't reconcile her expectations with her sense of calling: through his patience,

Mr Simpson gave her time to recognise that her expectations had no real claim on her. Because education is a development of students' connections with the whole world, it is an intrinsically healthy process. Mr Simpson was fulfilling a *pastoral* responsibility when nurturing Jenny's unique potential.

Mr Simpson's patience returns us to a point made by Buber. Whereas ethical behaviour or responsibility is normally seen as the duty of an autonomous subject, as the obligation of an I to an It, responsibility from an I–Thou perspective is the I's open response to a particular situation. Responsibility is about *being there* for Thou, not about fixing their life for them.

The constancy of Mr Simpson involved a courage that wasn't found in some of Jenny's other teachers. The teachers who panicked or lost patience with her were, strangely, over-identifying with her. Having perhaps taken too much pride in her success, they were afraid of having a personal responsibility when she got into trouble. Jenny became a problem to be solved and, in shifting responsibility to Jenny's parents and to Jenny herself, the teachers were insisting that she wasn't their problem. They abandoned her to save themselves; they abandoned her because they were too identified to be able to see her potential through the eyes of the I–Thou relation. This, then, is the danger for teachers whose care loses its particular teacherliness. If they become identified with the student's problems, they cannot help them reconnect with the world.

Just as there is a problem when teachers over-identify with their students, there is a problem when parents over-identify with their children. If parents try to remove all the discomforts that schooling brings, they will be setting themselves against the openness of learning. Parents need to give teacher and student the space and respect they need if they are to establish a productive relation, a relation that is different from that of parenting. Schools are where parents learn to let their children go. A parent told us:

Parents send their kids to school for education, but for the kids it's about being part of a group, about growing up. It's a different world. I wasn't a pushy parent. I preferred to talk to my daughter about school; it was her experience primarily. As a rule, I didn't think that my talking to teachers was appropriate. What mattered more was my daughter's response to them. My job was to help her reflect on what was going on for her.

The particularity of the teacher's care came out in our interviews with teachers who were themselves parents. They would not want to teach their own children, they said, because they could not care as parents and teachers at the same time. As Elizabeth Game put it, 'Your own child knows all the nooks and crannies of your personality, consciously or subconsciously, and that complicates the teacher–student relationship. The teacher needs to present themselves to a student much more cleanly'.

Elizabeth went on to explain:

Teachers and students need to focus on what that relationship is about, on the education rather than personal agendas. Teachers get on[to] shaky ground if they want to know too much about the student's personal life without the student volunteering it. As a teacher, you only get what's given to you. It's important for the student to know that your main interest is in the history of Crete, and not in the outcome of the football game on the weekend. You may mention that as you're leaving the class, but you don't want to step over that red line in class because it generally translates into a lack of respect. Students feel that the teacher isn't serious enough about what they're doing, and then for the students there is no seriousness either.

Elizabeth helps us resolve the impasse in the debates about the role of care in education. Teachers who do not care for students cannot educate, because they are unable to meet the students and address them in their particularity, I to Thou. They will be unable, also, to establish a classroom environment where students remain fearless when faced with the apparent risks that learning entails. Elizabeth would add, however, that teachers who do not educate do not really care, for in focusing on personal problems, they neither address the students as whole people nor encourage them to engage with the world.

LOVE'S HONESTY

Whereas I–It relations are desirous, the teacher and student in an I–Thou relation are responsive to each other, without any agenda or strategy. Because of its wholism, moreover, such a relation inclines to the truth. Raimond Gaita made this point by telling the story of how a teacher's love changed his life and engendered his love of learning and truth.

The story concerned a time when Raimond was in trouble at his Catholic high school because of his advocacy of Bertrand Russell's views on sex and sex education. Raimond described himself as being then more inclined 'to delinquency … than to study'. There was no love or respect in Raimond's relation with the school's headmaster, for both were using their knowledge and relationship to prove themselves. Desiring Raimond to become the sort of person who would affirm the correctness of his own life, the headmaster refused to see Raimond as he was. Raimond's reaction perpetuated this I–It logic: seeing Bertrand Russell as a way to reinforce himself in his struggles with authority, Raimond reduced his capacity to learn from either Russell or the headmaster.

The way out of this dilemma was through Martin Winkler, who was giving Raimond private lessons in German. Winkler had taught theology with Albert Schweitzer and worked as a Lutheran pastor, and so might have been expected to try to save Raimond from his delinquent ways. Winkler's gift, however, was to see beyond Raimond's defiance to his vulnerability and potential.

> [W]hen he learned about the cause of my trouble, he gave me a book to read—at home, I should say, because I was about to go there on vacation. *He's superficial. He doesn't understand what he attacks. But you might as well understand why you are in such trouble*, Winkler told me, when he handed me the book. The author he referred to was Russell; the book, *Why I am not a Christian*.

In giving Raimond a book which he himself didn't admire, Winkler was showing respect for Raimond as he was, regardless of any delinquency; he was also giving him the chance to read Russell with an open mind. This was an example, for Raimond, of how Winkler taught without pedagogic strategy.

For many years Raimond visited Winkler at his home. Rather than trying to teach his student anything, Winkler unselfconsciously put the things he loved in Raimond's way. He talked of books, he played Bach on the organ in his study. 'I was entranced by his untroubled confidence that he had revealed to me some of the great treasures of Western civilisation. It never occurred to me to ask why he did it because I knew, as everyone does, that people enjoy sharing what they love.'

Because Winkler did not define himself through positions, he did not force Raimond into them either. Winkler didn't try to impose Bach upon Raimond; Winkler simply demonstrated his love for Bach. This experience was, as Raimond said, 'a revelation': 'Winkler's love of Bach awakened the same love in me'. Through love, the treasures of Western civilisation directly entered Raimond's life, there in Winkler's study.

Raimond said that real love can be distinguished from its many false forms because of its connection with truth. He was referring to the way love suspends the desirous self: it is honest because it has no agenda. By teaching Raimond the difference between love and desire, Winkler taught him how to do honest, scholarly work; he taught him that intellectual rigour is a quality of heart. It is courageous (*coeur*: heart). Raimond couldn't have written *Romulus, My Father*, for example, except for Winkler's gift:

> I drew on [my love of Bach]—I needed it—when I wrote *Romulus, My Father*. Writing about things that affected me profoundly, I had to resist as much as possible all temptations to pathos or sentimentality if I was to see things clearly. ...
>
> Iris Murdoch ... said that understanding the reality of another person is a work of love, justice and pity. She meant, I think, that love, justice and pity are *forms* of understanding, rather than merely conditions which facilitate understanding—conditions like a clear head, a good night's sleep, an alcohol-free brain. Real love is hardheaded and unsentimental. When one rids oneself of sentimentality, pathos and similar failings, one allows justice, love and pity to do their *cognitive* work, their work of disclosing reality. Sometimes the full reality of another human being is visible only to love. To be truthful about the significance of the story I was telling—to be able to reveal the full humanity of my father even when he seemed utterly degraded by his illness, so much so that when I was a boy I once denied he was my father—I listened to Bach.

The humble simplicity of love allowed Raimond to reveal truth about his father that was beyond the reach of the subjectivity and objectivity of the I–It relation. It was a love, and a love of truth, that he learned from the love of his teacher.

Raimond is drawing attention to the fact that values—love, respect, humility—are more than a curriculum content to convey: they are the way someone like Winkler teaches. Education and knowledge are forms of relation. To know is to relate openly.

LOVE OF LEARNING

A parent told us that although her child was getting excellent academic results, she worried that he is not developing a love for the work. She highlighted, in this way, the difference between a desire for outcomes and a love of learning.

> My son approaches work as if it is something to be done quickly, with completion itself as the goal. Teachers haven't yet got across to him that what matters is the *way* you do it, doing it with logic, neatness, precision and interest, finding ways to do it better or differently yourself, going beyond the basic task. What's important isn't the end, but the reflective relationship with what you're doing and what more you can do with what you have done. He still needs to learn this.

Teachers insisted that more important than teaching a set curriculum is teaching this love of learning. But, they joked, you couldn't nominate *this* when listing outcomes expected of your classes. This joke reflects the discrepancy between classroom practices and educational institutions. As bureaucratic organisations, the latter have to define their aims in measurable terms in order to be accountable. Teachers, on the other hand, monitor progress by attending to the relational qualities of their classes.

From the perspective of the classroom, prescribed teaching outcomes present problems of desire. If outcomes are mistaken as the point of education, they limit students' potential. Students focused on ends are not fully engaged in the learning process; they ask the wrong questions, they comply with other people's answers. In Barbara Devlin's phrase, such students *just don't get* the point of education:

> Some students want a formulaic approach: *Tell me what to do and I'll do it.* If I look up a word in a dictionary, I occasionally hear a little voice, *You're supposed to be the English teacher.* They expect you to have all the answers. And I think that's very sad. It's very infrequent and it tends to be the kids who just don't get it, the kids who have a very utilitarian attitude to education. It's about getting your money's worth. Education is merely a stepping stone, a hurdle, a means to an end and I think that's really, really sad.
>
> I remember a particular student who accused me of not teaching him properly. If I were a proper teacher I wouldn't just circle the spelling errors in his work, I'd write in the correct spellings for him. I really want him to leave school with the sort of skills that he can put into practice, and if I correct his spelling for him, he's not going to get those benefits. That's not what it's about.

Because of their informality, Martin Winkler's lessons with Raimond weren't being institutionally assessed as the achievement of prescribed outcomes. He could easily eschew *pedagogical strategy*. Different challenges face teachers who work in institutional settings but still need to produce classroom environments that manifest the love of learning. They must bridge the two worlds of institution and classroom, protecting students from the pedagogic desires of the institution. As Barbara put it, 'I have to make sure my students are interested in what I teach them and that they progress in terms of their own learning. Bureaucracy is bureaucracy, and students need not worry about that. That's my worry'.

Good teachers, then, do not simply ignore institutional demands. They must know the set curriculum outcomes, but suspend the desire for these during class discussions. In this way they allow the outcomes to be rediscovered through an enquiry based on a love of learning. If teachers can't put love of learning as a goal, they can nevertheless inspire it by sharing their own love. This was the point made by Vicky Yannakouros when she told us how she went about teaching a love of learning.

It's tiny little things all day every day, and a lot of it's not even conscious stuff. I'll give an example. I've always been a huge believer in being really honest with children. We talk about everything. Discussion and questioning is just intrinsic, and listening to children question. Our outcome for this term is living things, and the other day we had a class on the differences between living and non-living things. I thought *OK, I'm going to try some ideas I heard in a presentation about philosophy for children*. I put the words Living and Non-Living up on the board and I said *I'm not going to tell you what they mean*. So then I put the children into groups to just talk and it was interesting because I heard these snippets of conversations and I thought *Oh my God! What are they talking about?* And then they came back and I asked them to tell me what they talked about. So they just brainstormed. And we wrote down all this stuff and … can I show you?! It's just fascinating.

At this point in the interview, Vicky jumped up and collected a pile of butcher's paper covered in lists, key words and questions, using it to explain the class's thought process.

And then the questions got really good: *I want to learn about the people who were first alive or the time before people were alive. Why are the dinosaurs dead or extinct? How did one person start off man, because now there are millions and millions of people around, so was there one person first? How did the first person come to earth? How did monkeys turn into people? What do bugs' bones look like? How did the caveman get alive?* [and so on.] So I just went, *Uh oh, right.* So I've since spoken to our teacher librarian and the high-school science teacher and we've started planning all sorts of stuff we can do together. I'm really excited about that because I figure I'm still covering the curriculum but I'm working with my kids and it's about what they want to do.

Vicky is teaching an outcome, yet she is doing so by teaching a love of learning. She is teaching her kindy class in the same respectful way Winkler taught Western civilisation to Raimond: through sharing what she loves. Like Winkler, Vicky doesn't teach strategically; through her own openness, she allows an I–Thou relation which makes everyone in her classroom aware of the wonder of the world. The world can be met as difference. This ethical relation makes learning and a love of learning inevitable.

The class's achievement is to meet the outcome: instead of the issues of *living things* feeling remote, they are now urgently relevant to the students' own lives. Their questions place their lives in a bigger context, and bring that new context close to home. This experience acknowledges them as people who participate in the world of knowledge, yet it also revitalises their sense of the mystery of who they are. Based on wonder, this is a learning process that doesn't end with a single outcome, and yet it addresses the required outcomes.

Like Winkler's, Vicky's love of learning is inspiring because of its humility. Because Vicky is always learning how to teach, and because she loves learning, she is as excited as the students about the way her teaching experiment unfolds. She doesn't put on a show of enthusiasm; her joy in their questions is entirely authentic. When she looks at their eager faces she sees in them a potential that they share. And because she is open, when the students look at her they see their own potential. This is how wonderful life can be! More than any words of praise, her joy shows the students what they are capable of doing.

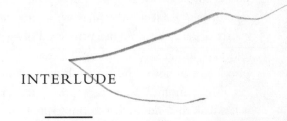

INTERLUDE

———

Raimond Gaita: Loving Your Subject

Raimond Gaita, a philosopher and writer, is concerned with the way teaching is corrupted if it is focused on the teacher's desires and goals. According to him, teaching is a form of love. Teachers find their own needs met by devoting themselves to students and to the subjects taught.

Only something like the concept of vocation, I think, will enable one adequately to characterise the importance of love to a deepened conception of what it is to care for a subject for its own sake.

Reflecting later on Winkler, on what he gave me and so many others, I realised that the value of the teaching life cannot itself be taught. It can only be shown, but of course, only to those who have eyes to see. It is revealed through a teacher's manner of teaching when it is determined by her attentive obedience to the disciplines of her subject. This is why teachers who set out to inspire have their attention in the wrong place and are too distracted from their subject to be able to offer anything deep no matter how many hearts they set afire. Just as charity is corrupt unless it is motivated by the needs of another rather than by the desire to do something charitable, so teachers inspire their students into a proper love of what they are doing by the manner of their attention to their subject rather than by setting out to inspire them.

A teacher's vocation, her privileged obligation, is, as Plato saw, and as Winkler taught me by his example, to initiate her pupils into a worthy love. There is nothing finer that one human being can do for another. Mostly, for over-determined reasons, teaching is less than this and there is nothing much to be done about it. But it remains the highest standard in the light of which teachers may describe and judge what they do and in whose light students may recognise the treasure which their studies can offer them.

CHAPTER FOUR

A PASSION FOR LEARNING

PASSION

As a young primary school teacher, Sharon Cheers was inspired by a senior colleague, Alison Pegus, and it was the dynamic of Alison's classroom that particularly impressed her:

> As soon as you walked into Alison's classroom, you could tell it was working. There was lots of movement, lots of different things happening, but there was still a sense of calm. I suppose her passion came through everything she did.

In using the word 'passion', Sharon was echoing everyone we spoke to. Teachers who change lives are invariably characterised by their passion and their enthusiasm.

> What good teachers have is passion. The spark. Sharing their passion. Kids pick up on their excitement, and that makes them curious.

> She was so enthusiastic, she was just such an inspiration to me, and I think she ignited something in me.

There was a teacher who made a big difference in my life, who really turned me on to English. It was his enthusiasm. That's the memory that comes to me immediately.

Although it is often assumed that classroom energy comes from the force of the teacher's personality, this view fails to appreciate the relationality of true passion and enthusiasm. 'Passion' is a word commonly confused with 'desire', but Sharon's insistence on the significance of classroom atmospherics indicates its basis in an I–Thou relation. Genuine passion needs to be distinguished from a show of passion that is based on the logic of I–It.

Passion, enthusiasm and inspiration are all concepts from religious tradition, pointing to a soulful vitality that emerges when people come together. The hum of the classroom involves everyone, yet is beyond the control of even the teacher: something *happens*, without anyone making it happen. This is an understanding of spirituality that places it within the ordinary world, for the classroom spirit comes from these children and this teacher at this moment.

GIVING AND TAKING ENERGY

Energy is only given when it can be received. When teachers try to supply an energy that students cannot receive, the effects are unhealthy. Imagine a conscientious teacher worried about the students' ability to cope with the curriculum. 'I sometimes look at my kids,' a teacher told us, 'and feel overwhelmed by how much they need to learn'. The students are now seen for their insecurity rather than their potential. Moreover, this overprotective concern with the students' weakness awakens in teachers their own fear of inadequacy. Their response is panic, a feeling of exhaustion masked by adrenalin.

This feeling of inadequacy is common throughout the educational system. At university, for example, lecturers often go into overdrive to fill the gap between what students know and what they need to know. As a lecture draws to an end, they speak faster, rushing between PowerPoint slides before students have had a chance to read them. No longer aware of the students' ability to comprehend, such teachers are focused entirely on what they need to say to fulfil their obligations.

If students *feel* lectured, they feel disrespected, and usually respond with bored disengagement or defiance. In course evaluations, they talk of lecturers who go too fast, lecturers who go too slow, lecturers who go on and on, lecturers whose lessons are irrelevant, and lecturers who just don't care.

A more complex dynamic arises if teachers are charismatic, delivering high-adrenalin lectures that impress and excite students. Proud to be associated with such teachers, students may feel energised by their desire to be equally knowledgeable. Yet this thrill can't last. When students put teachers on pedestals, they put themselves down. Although temporarily motivated by the teacher's virtuosity, they become exhausted and fearful when alone in the presence of their work. Overwhelmed by their teacher's prowess, they are also overwhelmed by their distance from this achievement.

Whether students are bored, defiant or star-struck, these dynamics have the same ethical basis. Teachers who see students in terms of lack are disrespecting students, by measuring them against desired outcomes, and are overrating themselves by taking personal responsibility for getting the students to measure up. The teacher's pride, however, turns easily to a sense of failure; students are insatiable when they are too anxious to receive what the class offers. Faced with students who seem resourceless, teachers feel their energy being drained. The infinitude of the I–Thou relation is reduced to a parsimonious awareness of quantities. As Sharon Cheers said,

> When you've got some kids that just take, that drains a teacher's energy. I think teachers can burn out very, very easily because teachers give of their time. You give, give, give and give and then the holidays come and then you collapse.

It often happens, then, that teachers try to supply the classroom energy. But this is a sign of relational and institutional malaise. When the classroom is *working*, Sharon feels that she receives more than she gives: 'The special moments and the giving you receive have an immense impact, so ultimately *they* are changing my life and keeping the sense of wonder alive for me—indeed a precious gift'. Sharon explained with a story:

> It's the little things. For example, Year 7 has been designing board games and Year 4 were the clientele. There's a Year 7 boy who has Asberger's Syndrome, so he finds socialising quite difficult. He's very quirky. And anyway he had made the most elaborate and amazing board game around his area of interest, which was dinosaurs, and he came down to the classroom, and the Year 4s got to play the game. When someone would have to move their piece, he'd jump in to move it for them. So I said, *Trust them, they will play it really well. Just let them do it.* And he sat there, and you should have seen his smile. Because if you see him, a lot of the time he's on his own, and he tries to connect with his peers but he can't. But today he's got something that he's created and people are playing it, and all of a sudden he's just grinning. And that I think is very interesting. And now I'm going to cry. And he's not even a student

of mine. When kids do something that you know has been difficult for them, those are the beautiful moments.

When students attribute the passion of a lively classroom to teachers, it may be because they are not aware of their own contribution: they assume the energy they feel is coming from the teacher, but actually a more awesome and relational process is at work. Just as you cannot point to a relation, you cannot point to the source of the enthusiasm of a classroom.

THE ENERGY OF ENCOUNTER

Passion, as its etymology implies, is an energy that involves passivity. It is something you receive, something that moves you; it is the compassion of patient devotion. Emerson contrasts this genuine passion with the 'military hurry' that characterises much education. In this rush, students become masses, and their particular educational needs are overlooked.

Now the correction of this quack practice is to adopt the pace of Nature. Her secret is patience. Do you know how the naturalist learns all the secrets of the forest …? His secret is patience; he sits down, and sits still. … By dint of obstinate sitting still, reptile, fish, bird and beast, which all wish to return to their haunts, begin to return. He sits still; if they approach, he remains passive as the stone he sits upon. They lose their fear. They have curiosity too about him … By and by they come swimming, creeping and flying towards him. … Can you not wait for [the student], as Nature and Providence do? Can you not keep for his mind and ways, for his secret, the same curiosity you give to the squirrel, snake, rabbit, and the sheldrake and the deer? He has a secret; wonderful methods in him;

he is—every child—a new style of man; give him time
and opportunity.

Emerson is saying that teachers needs the faith of the naturalist.
They need to wait patiently, approaching students by allowing
students time to approach them. When students praise their
teachers for their passion, they are alluding, then, to the faith that
teachers have brought to the classroom. Teachers know that each
class will eventually find its unique energy.

Sharon Cheers told us that engaged learning cannot occur until
she and the students know each other, as members of a class that
has taken on a life of its own. Until then, her lessons are not lessons
for *this* class. They do not address the needs of these particular
students. So Sharon attends closely, looking for the change signalled
by a smile, a warmth, a relaxation, a change in body language.
There will be a moment of *getting it* when the class comes together
and comes alive. Once this lively relationship exists, students are
able to receive what is being given to them, and giving is no
longer a drain on the teachers' energy:

> There comes a time when I say *I've got them now*. And
> when I feel that I've got them, I feel that I know what
> they're going to need. That's the thing about term one.
> You create a unit, you're organised, but you don't really
> know the kids, so you're constantly shifting things. You've
> got to get it to the stage where they can work together as
> a whole and accept the difference in each other. That's
> when you can see amazing opportunities.
>
> I suppose once you've got them, you can relax. You can
> give and you get back and it becomes this sort of reci-
> procal relationship of knowing and understanding, and it's
> meaningful. It's an openness. If they're giving, they're also
> open to feedback, they're open to change. They get to a

point where they say *Oh yeah, I've got it*. There's a sense of confidence. It's when you're explaining something and they smile or they look at you. It's those funny moments that keep you going. That's the giving. That's when you see something happening in the classroom that's really exciting. I suppose you just sort of ride this energy and that momentum carries you through.

The student's smile of *getting it* is simultaneously a receiving of knowledge and a getting of the classroom relationship. Moreover, when Sharon describes the smile as an open giving, she is drawing attention to the way giving and receiving are simultaneous within relationships. The student is unselfconsciously giving thanks for what they have received. In giving of themselves, they receive what they need; in accepting what they need, they give the teacher what she needs to carry on. There is a gift but you cannot say who is giving what. This logic of giving and receiving is the experience of grace: what each person needs is effortlessly provided if people are open with each other. Sharon's metaphor for grace might be taken from surfing: *you just sort of ride this energy and that momentum carries you through*. People are at once still and on the edge, being drawn on, in fascination.

How Passion Helps Learning

This is how Julie McCrossin described her life-changing teacher, Mrs Miller:

> Passion, patience and boundless personal relationship with each girl, they're the three qualities of a great teacher like Mrs Miller. The most passionate, erudite, curious hunger for learning: that was the spirit I got from Enid Miller and it's alive and well.

Mrs Miller's *passion* was her genuine love of reading, literature and performance: 'she wasn't bunging it on, she was absolutely authentic: she really loved Donne and Shakespeare'. Mrs Miller's *patience* was evident in the faith she had in the girls' ability to learn through performance: she allowed them time to find their own ways into the roles and hence the plays. Her *boundless personal relationship with each girl* manifested her respect and compassion: 'she had the ability to make everyone feel special. She really cared; that's the human connection'. These three qualities came together in the curiosity that characterised Mrs Miller's classroom. Julie said:

> What I mean by really teaching is the ability to arouse, to stimulate to learn, so that the student is made curious and wants to take independent additional action. They're enthusiastic, electrified. Good teachers have a gift, a vocation, and the core of it for me is that they want you to learn as much as they want to learn themselves. In fact it goes deeper than that. Mrs Miller thought she could learn from students. She felt how Julie and the others responded to the trauma of Lady Macbeth and in this way she could experience the trauma of Lady Macbeth afresh.

Mrs Miller's classroom combined passion with patience, movement with stillness, exuberance with respectful attention. It had the calm energy of Martin Winkler's Bach-filled study: a new world is dawning, and time stands still in a state of wonder. By suspending the trajectory of the desirous self, passion returns students' attention to the task at hand. Patient and receptive, it provides the time students need if they are to mature.

Think of Mrs Miller's students performing Shakespeare in class. They aren't rushing to interpret Shakespeare, and they're not distracted by the prospect of exams. They simply devote themselves to the particular lines of speech before them, playing with them until they ring true. When the lines resound with the vitality of a full body, who is providing the energy? Is it Shakespeare? Julie? Lady Macbeth? Western civilisation? Mrs Miller? Who is active here and who is passive? It is the unanswerability of these questions that gives passion its cognitive power. When it is passionate, the work of Mrs Miller's students will be true to both Shakespeare and the students. This authenticity will be the proof that lessons have been well learned.

In her account of Mrs Miller, Julie several times linked enthusiasm and passion with curiosity. Open to receive what lessons have to offer, interested to see what they will learn about Lady Macbeth and what she will teach them about themselves, students face their day with faith and hope. This is not a curiosity that seeks satisfaction but one that enjoys being part of Shakespeare's universality. It is not faith in any *thing*, or hope for any identifiable outcome; it is acceptance that the only life available is the one that unfolds from here and now. This class matters. It is not a lesson about life, it is life.

The patience of the passionate classroom is, then, a form of presence. Students and teachers know that everything they need is already here; they know too that what they need will not be what they could have anticipated. Awaited answers, Buber says, cannot be received. The answer comes

> not from a distance but from the air round about me, noiselessly. ... Really it did not come; it was there. It had been there—so I may explain it—even before my [question]: there it was, and now, when I laid myself open to it, it let itself be received by me. ... If I were to report with what I heard it I should have to say 'with every pore of my body'. (Buber, 2002: 3)

A PASSION FOR TEACHING

If teaching isn't experienced as a relation, it presents a frightening prospect. Many teachers privately fear that they lack attributes that other teachers have. *I can't make jokes. I'm not an entertainer. So what am I to do?* In this state, teachers don't realise that students will help provide whatever the class needs, if they can see how they are needed.

Julie speaks of *the teacher's gift or vocation*. This gift is not a personal largesse, it is the ability to be in an I–Thou relation where giving and receiving are simultaneous. In other words, the teacher's gift is their ability to receive from the classroom what they need. The teacher with vocation is someone who knows they need to teach.

Julie drew attention to this question of teachers' needs. Following her account of the three qualities that made Mrs Miller a great teacher, Julie added a description of Mrs Miller's idiosyncrasies:

> And the final thing I will say is that she was just hilariously idiosyncratic. She was clearly a smoker, desperately thin. Looking back, her agitation must have been a desire to smoke. And she had very overt phobias. She was terrified of birds and if a bird ever flew past a classroom, Mrs Miller almost had a nervous breakdown. That only endeared her to us more. She was a very quirky individual, Mrs Miller.
>
> It's a miracle in a way, her personal passion, her knowledge of her material, her love of learning and teaching were all so strong that even though she was very lined and old, battered by life, she could reach across this extraordinary gap to these teenagers.

The discrepancy between the agitated and quirky individual and the passionate and patient teacher tell us about the transformative power of classroom relations. Through their relation, the students gave Mrs Miller qualities that were not available to her on her own. When the students experienced Mrs Miller in full flight, discussing Donne or Shakespeare, they didn't look at her age or lined face: she met them across the extraordinary age gap because she wasn't limited by such definitions.

We imagine that Mrs Miller knew her vocation because she felt blessed by this transformative power. The calmness of the classroom allowed her to accept her sometime agitation; she probably had as bemused a relation with her quirks as the students did. They were simply part of who she was. Even these vulnerabilities had their place, *only endearing her to students more*. Mrs Miller did not have to set out to entertain the students because, if she was real with them, humour naturally found its way into the classroom. Mrs Miller trusted that students would appreciate her uniqueness just as she respected theirs.

Vocation involves acceptance. It is what you accept and where you're accepted. Vilma Rotellini made this point when joking about the way her students need to correct her:

> Sometimes I want things to be perfect straightaway and they feel comfortable enough to say *But Mrs Rotto, we can't do that now, we need more time to do it*. And then I know that I have set unrealistic goals and I want them to do it too quickly so I have to pull back. Or I'm judgemental sometimes. I say things to the children about not being judgemental and then they'll remember it and come back and say *Now you're being judgemental* and I will say *You're absolutely right*. Sometimes we teach them what we ourselves need to be learning. The modelling goes both ways.

The point isn't that teaching is therapy or that good teachers are successful despite their vulnerabilities. Vulnerabilities *allowed* Vilma and Mrs Miller to teach; as part of the way they were, they were the way they entered the classroom. To be real with students, teachers have to accept both their strengths and weaknesses; they enter the class with humility because they know that they need the students' help.

Although the words 'calling' and 'vocation' sound quaint beside the desirous vocabulary of 'choice', 'decision' and 'career', interviewees insisted on the vocation of good teachers. As an awareness of where one is needed *and* needs to be, calling takes teachers beyond the alienating choices of desire. Producing the wholeness of give-and-take, and providing the serene energy of passion, calling places teachers and students exactly where they need to be to *get it*.

The teacher's call is not a once-in-a-lifetime message from on high: it is simply a compassionate openness to the signs present every day, in every classroom. When Sharon Cheers is surprised by a smile or a look from a student, it is her calling that she hears.

———

Michael Kirby:
Lessons Not Forgotten

Michael Kirby, Judge of the High Court of Australia, is a great advocate for public education. When we asked him to tell us about a life-changing teacher, he insisted on noting all of his teachers, one by one. All left a mark on him. This is a story of an unusual mark, left when a teacher blotted his copybook.

Then I went off to the Summer Hill system and I had Mr Gorringe, Mr Tennant, Mr Gibbons. Mr Tennant, my teacher in sixth class, had a motor-car accident so Mr Gibbons, the headmaster, a small, nuggetty, somewhat volatile man who had fought in the First World War (as many of the teachers had at that time) took over. He was the only teacher who caned me. I still remember the injustice of the occasion. I had spilt ink. In those days we had inkwells and I had somehow dislodged the inkwell and ink fell onto my green-covered departmental exercise book. I had torn out a number of the pages in order to remove the stain. Mr Gibbons, who had a marvellous sense of avoirdupois, picked up the book and immediately said *This book is light. You have torn pages out of a departmental exercise book. Do you realise this is the King's property? You have removed part of the King's property. Come out and put up your hand.* And I said *But, but, but.* He would have no explanations, no excuses and I was caned twice, literally for blotting my copybook. To this day, I am more attentive to arguments about injustice than most people. I believe that's because, seared onto my consciousness, is the horror that one day I will do to others what Mr Gibbons did to me. He was of course a very good headmaster. He had to run a school that had both the Opportunity C classes, which were for high IQ students, and general classes. That wasn't an easy thing to do. But it was he who announced under the big tree which is still in front of the Summer Hill Public School in Sydney, that I had been selected to go to Fort Street High School, which was what I wanted to do.

CHAPTER FIVE

———

THE IMPORTANCE
OF AUTHORITY

How Authority Becomes Perverse

Responsibility is understood in different ways, leading to different forms of authority. When responsibility is seen as open response to the other, authority is organic, emerging from the particular relation. When responsibility is seen as responsibility *for* the other, as regulation, authority manifests fear of the openness of relationships. In the latter case, where responsibility is unresponsive, the interests of the authority are substituted for the interests of others: authority becomes perverse, irresponsibly removed from those it desires to regulate.

During our interviews, we heard many stories of authority gone perverse. Among teachers and parents there was a widespread sense of despair at being unheard.

I was working late one night and someone in authority passed by and said *What are you doing so late?* I said *I'm writing my teaching program for the principal* and they said *Shouldn't you be writing your program for you*? I said <u>*No*</u>, <u>*my program is my kids*</u>. I got into trouble over that and was invited in for a chat. They thought my attitude was wrong. They seem to think you teach a program whereas I think you teach children.

They came up with this stupid rule a few years ago. They told primary school teachers that we weren't allowed to touch the children any more. Well, I may as well give up teaching now. If a child is upset, how could you not hold them? It seems as if the school is more interested in protecting itself rather than protecting the children.

Education is the process of learning, and we do assessment to check how the process is going. But some people turn it all around. Here's a recent example. The process of writing an essay should be a learning experience, so I get students to write multiple drafts: I give them feedback and so do their friends. And then at the assessment stage, there's more feedback. As it happens, these essays don't get plagiarised: we're all too involved and the final essays are all different. But other academics set essay topics that obviously imply that there's a correct answer, and of course some students find they can plagiarise. So you know what happens? To get rid of plagiarism, the faculty wants us to get rid of final essays and replace them with exams that offer no feedback at all, just a grade.

The principal was so patronising, you couldn't believe it really. Even though my daughter was only twelve, she noticed instantly that all he had were the words. An example was the agreement every new student had to sign. It was corporate management 101. They had to promise to do all the right things. It was a simulation of an equal relationship and came with all the pseudo words. All that contract stuff assumes that twelve year olds have capacities they don't have. It's entirely inappropriate. This man had the PR words to get promoted, but he still didn't know how to relate to children.

In each of these cases, authority has lost a sense of its role in providing support for relationships. In trying to calculate and regulate relations, it interferes with the strange uncontrollable chemistry on which they rely. Rather than protecting learning relations, this authority is concerned primarily to show that it is not responsible for any outcomes that don't match expectations.

Because perverse authority shows no faith in teachers, it leaves them feeling both unsupported and undermined in their vocation. If education is to fulfil its role, teachers must be allowed to teach. They need the time and opportunity to establish a creative, reliable learning environment in the classroom. They need from their leaders the same nurturing authority that their students need from them.

RELIABLE AUTHORITY

If education is a relational process, and teachers cannot unilaterally generate a creative learning experience, they nevertheless have a crucial role in establishing the conditions within which relationships can flourish. Their responsiveness provides the safety of a reliable authority. Vicky Yannakouros, for example, devotes the whole of term one to establishing the routines that make her students feel physically and emotionally safe. Without this safety, she told us emphatically, no child can learn:

> Once you've established this feeling of safety, you can vary your teaching mode. The class hums along. So I'm not advocating running a militant classroom where children

can't breathe without putting their hand up. On the contrary, I think those routines in a sense free them.

I say to the children at the beginning of the year *We don't have rules but we have a question: Is that safe? It's not safe if it hurts your body or someone else's body, your feelings or someone else's feelings, or our school property.* A five year old knows straightaway whether something is safe or not. With play, for example, I'd say *How can we change your game to make it safe?* So they're making those decisions; they'll say *We can do this instead and we can do that.* So the whole safety issue is giving them a reflective ability.

Vicky believes that the generation of this order is the most difficult task facing teachers. Yet, once it is established, classroom management becomes inconspicuous, able to rely on patterns of conduct integrated into the learning environment. Without this reliable authority, students feel abandoned, too anxious to learn.

Stephanie Alexander, restaurateur and author, told a story about the disorder that prevails where there is no reliable authority. When she was eleven, there was no school in her area for Year 7, and the children were bussed every day to a church hall one-and-a-quarter hours away. They had their lessons there, completely detached from any other school.

The most significant thing was that there was absolutely no authority. There were two teachers, both straight out of teacher's college, who had to deal with these fifty children, who were just floating around really, not knowing what they were doing. The teachers were weak and the kids just went mad. It was a real *Lord of the Flies*. Nice kids turned into little delinquents. Children came into the classrooms via windows; they roamed at lunchtime; they found wells; they picked fruit off trees. They just walked over those two teachers. I remember the worst thing I did, and I'd always been a very dutiful child, I threw a pen at the teacher because he was presenting a very passive bottom. I threw it like a dart, a pitiful thing to do. And anyway, one teacher had a nervous breakdown. She disappeared and was never seen again.

Everything about this story speaks of abandonment. The students' delinquency was a sign of the distress they felt in the absence of boundaries to hold them: *they were just floating around, not knowing what they were doing*. Rather than bringing the children satisfaction, frantic activity only left them terrified of the chaotic possibilities they found within themselves. These delinquents were, as Stephanie said, *pitiful*.

When Stephanie says that the teachers *had no authority*, she is speaking of the failure of a relation. Without the patterns of conduct that would support the learning and teaching relation, the teachers would have been as distressed as the students. We imagine them alternating between appeasement and heavy-handed discipline, trying desperately to find some mode that would bring relief. They were probably frustrated and scared by their own failure. Everyone in the classroom, then, was left to their own devices, with too many decisions to make and little confidence in their ability to make them.

The woman who rescued this class from its abandonment was the most influential teacher in Stephanie's life:

In the place of the teacher who had the nervous breakdown, they sent a teacher who I later discovered had just come from England. Her name was Mary T. She was a deserted wife, she had a young child, she desperately needed to earn her living and she had teaching qualifications. She was also exceedingly cross-eyed, which amused the children no end on day one. She came down on them like 17 000 tons of bricks. She just kept fabulous order throughout the day, by sheer force of will. She didn't beat anybody, though she probably made people stand outside; she certainly was not prepared to tolerate bad behaviour of any sort.

Mary was actually a brilliant maths and English teacher, and she taught that whole year and transformed what was really a shocking situation into a bearable situation.

She had an enormous impact on me, and went on being a friend for years after we left school. Mary always had this rich worldliness; she was just a very, very strong personality. She loved theatre, and was very theatrical; she had a great number of gay male friends; she had all this social life, which was very unusual, I might add, for the 1950s. And she went to the theatre in town and had dinner parties—loved a glass of wine.

So Mary was a great mentor, she was a model; she also had a great sense of humour and she really treated us like people. But she often said in later years how appalled she was when she first came to our classroom and saw these eleven year olds who were absolutely out of control, who didn't know what they were doing or why they were there. They were supposed to learn.

Stephanie talks of *weak teachers*. Too dependent on students for their own sense of worth, weak teachers are unable to see students as they truly are. It is not generally understood that militant and laissez-faire teachers are alike in this identification; both are too frightened to *relate* to students. In both modes, teachers protect themselves by distancing students, refusing to genuinely *respond* to them.

By contrast, Mary T's strength lay in her courage. She could sympathise with the students—her heart went out to *these eleven year olds who didn't know what they were doing or why they were there*—but she didn't over-identify with them or see them only as a reflection on her. Consequently, even though their behaviour was *out of control*, Mary didn't panic and didn't try to unilaterally control the students as a weak teacher would. Her dramatic intervention was simply a first step in establishing the conditions of classroom order. She knew from experience that if she stood firm and waited with patience, the classroom would organise *itself* around and through her. Mary's trust in classroom dynamics was a faith in relationship, a trust in what she could do *with* her students.

When Stephanie refers to Mary as a *great mentor, a model*, she is pointing to Mary's modelling of a life of faith. Her reliability was not self-reliance but a devotion to the teacher's vocation. In recognising her devotion to the service of teaching, students also recognised her authority to guide them. They intuitively knew that her work was not self-interested.

In Stephanie's account, then, Mary's punishments were never personal or vindictive; it was the behaviour that was intolerable, not the students themselves. Mary offered the boundaries and acceptance that the students needed. In refusing to tolerate disrespectful acts, she reassured culprits that she knew they were capable of more, while reassuring other students that there was an order upon which they could rely. Her aim was not to prescribe proper behaviour but to encourage the open-hearted participation of each student.

In place of the distressing arbitrariness of their previous situation, students found safety and hope in Mary's *fabulous order*. Stephanie alludes to this when she speaks of Mary's *rich worldliness*. The spirit that students saw in her was a promise that there were things in the world worth doing. Just as Mary had found meaning and liveliness through her place in the world, so too would her students. Stephanie was particularly struck by this at high school, where she encountered Mary again, this time in the company of supportive colleagues:

> We happened to have six or eight teachers who were really dedicated to building a strong spirit in the school. They enjoyed each other and socialised quite a lot themselves. There seemed to be a lot of intellect among them. They saw themselves as setting up something, setting up a school. So there was very much a great call among them.

When the adult Stephanie speaks of her joy in respecting food and serving others, when she teaches this through her restaurants and books, we can feel the spirit of Mary T and her colleagues.

CLASSROOM FORMALITY

Once a classroom has come to life, the teacher's authority is embedded in the formality of everyday rituals and routines. Whereas imposed routines seem boring and repetitive, the formal routines of a trustworthy environment support creative risk-taking. They allow students and teachers to be open with each other and give each class the opportunity to develop its unique character.

According to physics teacher Kym Lawry, the teacher's authority allows students to focus on the process of learning itself rather than being distracted by exam anxieties. He said:

> We now very carefully prescribe exactly what the assessment is going to be, exactly what the criteria are, and I think that has benefit, but it also encourages the students to focus more on the assessments than the other things that go on. If the students are confident that you have a

clear understanding of the assessment in the subject, they won't be too focused narrowly on the exam. I'm less focused simply on the performance of my students in exams as I become a more experienced teacher.

In her interview, Jenny Oliver gave the student's perspective on this aspect of authority:

High school was a troublesome time for me. I took the weight of the HSC on my shoulders—the whole angst thing. One of the things that helped was that Mr Simpson's maths teaching was so regular. He was so constant. I can remember we'd walk in and there were mentals. Then he would go into checking homework—we'd do that. Then we'd have a little talk about a new concept. Then we'd do examples—I can remember it so clearly. Then we'd start the homework and also—rain, hail, whatever—if we wanted to see him at lunchtime for help, he was there without fail. In the morning, at recess, at lunchtime, without fail. I come back to that word 'reassurance'. It felt supportive, rather than boring. If you create that calm, supportive, anxious-free zone, the doors are open. It encourages that risk-taking.

Jenny's trust in the classroom routines was based on her acceptance of her teacher's authority. Because Mr Simpson's greater experience gave him a better sense of what the curriculum required, and of what Jenny could do, the steadiness of his schedules soothed her *angst*. Instead of being distracted by the future, she could focus on the task before her: when they were doing maths mentals, *that* was all they were doing. Because of its stillness, the classroom became a sanctuary in Jenny's life.

The logic of this *calm, supportive, anxious-free zone* is often mis-understood. People assume that creative work involves personal expression and confessional intimacy. Such an environment, however, makes people too self-conscious to get out of themselves. On the contrary, it is an interested impersonality that allows students to explore the aspects of their lives that elude their self-images.

Nick Jose highlighted this point. Talking about his poetry classes with Mr Schubert, Nick insisted that it was their academic rigour and formality that allowed the boys to find themselves through the truth of the poems:

> As sixteen-year-old boys, we found it incredibly difficult to express what we had inside. If Mr Schubert had been too intimate with us or too informal, I think we would have found it crippling. But by having this formal structure, it allowed us to get past our reserve; if we thought we were doing academic work, we could write about a love poem without becoming paralysed.

Nick's analyses of love poems resonated with his life, but he was never required to define himself in the writing process. He could hold open possibilities, in himself and in the poetry. Because they knew each other directly, as I knows Thou, they knew more than to reach conclusions about each other. Likewise, although Nick was fully engaged in his work, its formality helped him avoid becoming personally identified with it. Far from enforcing uniformity, classroom formality was a guarantee that Nick's difference would be respected. He could be open without fear that others would be overfamiliar.

In this formal environment, assessment processes become learning experiences. Because it is the academic work that is being assessed, students can avoid feeling pride or shame, and teachers can avoid censoring their responses for the students' sakes.

When formality is respected, mistakes become the way to learning rather than a failure of learning; they are reason for optimism rather than despair. Jenny is alluding to this healthy relation to assessment when she uses the phrase *without fail*.

Contrary to popular assumptions, then, it is respectful formality that allows teachers and students to be there for each other. If teachers try to become the students' friends, teaching relationships become expressions of personal preferences, and students' attention shifts from their work to pursuit of the teacher's approval. In such a situation, students can no longer trust that their work is being read honestly.

AUTHORITY WITH LOVE

In his book *Authority*, Richard Sennett distinguishes between authority with and authority without love. Through loving authority people give and receive the support they need to live creatively. This is a relation based on the directness of response, the honesty of love and the toughness of care. In contrast, authority without love is an authoritarian repression of creative capacities, a relation without responsive responsibility.

Drusilla Modjeska's account of her school life relied on this distinction between authority with and without love. Her secondary school, which she described as regimented and stiff, represented the latter. The school offered no support or acknowledgement when Drusilla's mother disappeared into a psychiatric hospital. 'With all those rules and regulations, there was nothing holding about that school.' It left her feeling simultaneously constricted and abandoned. Drusilla contrasted this with her earlier experience at Daneshill Prep School, where Miss Vallance was the headmistress. There must have been rules at Daneshill, Drusilla said, but she doesn't remember them. Instead she remembers the calm sense of order upon which school life relied.

One of her clearest memories was of the young, female, university-educated teachers having 'a lively life' outside class hours. While the girls were playing about in the school grounds, teachers might be playing tennis. There was fluency and freedom in their lives, and a sense of graceful order in their relations. Miss Vallance had authority for these teachers as well as for the students, but it was an authority that allowed people to thrive. Because students' lives were, Drusilla said, 'contiguous but different to the teachers' lives', students saw in the teachers their own promise.

One of the venerated formalities at Daneshill was bedtime:

> I remember a summer evening. There were six of us in the dorm above Miss Vallance's sitting room. It was summer and light, and we were leaping around and thumping on the floor when we were supposed to be in bed. She came up to see us. She wasn't cross. She just took two of us downstairs and gave us an orange juice. While we were drinking, we could hear the noise upstairs. We'd had no idea of how bad it was; we were shocked. Miss Vallance said, *This is my quiet time of the day without you girls.* We were really sorry and understood that she needed that quiet time because she'd been so engaged with us through the day.

When Miss Vallance reminded the girls that their floor was her ceiling, she showed how the levels of hierarchy were connected at Daneshill. This order was organic rather than imposed. At a regimented school, students might give lip service to the principal's authority without feeling responsibility or ethical obligation. At Daneshill, the girls couldn't hide from their responsibilities because they were implicated in the authority of the headmistress. They were learning about values; they were learning about courage and response.

Miss Vallance had a gift for running the place without enforcing rules, but she was quite tough; she didn't let you off the hook. When she took us downstairs to hear the noise upstairs she was insisting on the relationship. She wouldn't let us turn her into an authority figure to be dismissed. Instead we had to think about the implications of our behaviour on her.

Miss Vallance didn't have to impose her authority because it grew from her caring relation with the girls. In this case, then, Miss Vallance only had to let the noisy students hear what they were doing.

The healthy character of a loving authority was evident in Miss Vallance's response to Drusilla's family crisis:

When my mother went into the hospital in May and my father was all over the shop, my life just stopped. Everything stopped. But, unlike the school I went on to that September, there was no sense of shame. Miss Vallance accepted this family catastrophe as part of life; there was no secret about it. She drew a thread through this terrible thing and kept a sense of the future alive for me.

Miss Vallance's ability to face Drusilla's predicament without panic allowed Drusilla to face it too. When Drusilla had nothing else, it was her place in Daneshill that gave her life a sense of order and continuity. The crisis was acknowledged as part of Drusilla's life, but only part. Life went on at school. Even today, Drusilla recognises that her capacity for spontaneity relies on the resilience she learned from the reliability of the order that Miss Vallance embodied.

THE TEACHER'S AURA

Good teachers, like Miss Vallance, are always more than themselves. They are the incarnations of traditions and cultures, and carriers of learning environments. There is an aura about them, evidenced in the way ex-students continue to refer to them with honorifics like Miss or Mr. Without this aura, students cannot learn.

Michael Kirby, Judge of the High Court of Australia, told us a story that shows how this aura works.

> When I think of Fort Street [School] I think of the play night when there were teachers whom you were always just a little bit afraid of, in the sense that there was quite strong discipline at the school. I remember the play days and Mr Westlake. He used to take the school assembly. He was very dapper, rather elegant, but quite military in his bearing and in his commands. You always looked on him with a certain degree of awe and fear. But on play day he was putting the greasepaint on you and putting a false moustache on you and suddenly I saw he was quite a warm man. He was trying to get me ready to get in front of the lights and tread the boards and say my Shakespeare. I found that, actually, he had a very merry smile, which came as a tremendous shock to me as a person who had only ever seen him in assembly.
>
> I wouldn't say that the sense of awe is one of being overawed or frightened. That was not the ethos of Fort Street. It was a democratic community, so far as schools were democratic. ... But Mr Westlake was a particular teacher because he took the assembly. ... I'd never got to know the human side of him as you do if you have a teacher as your teacher. I always saw him as the school assembly marshal. Then suddenly I found he was a man with twinkling eyes. ... It never left my brain.

Michael was moved by the apparent disparity between the awe and fear that Mr Westlake inspired at assembly and the merry smile he offered backstage on play night. This was a moment of renewed appreciation, a double take that revealed the aura of loving authority beneath the authority that had seemed remote. Mr Westlake could not be reduced to one thing: he was both a merry smile and a commanding voice.

The merry smile allowed Michael to participate in Mr Westlake's authority, rather than feeling subject to it. Mr Westlake and he were both carriers of the school ethos, so that in respecting Mr Westlake, Michael felt he was respecting himself. Mr Westlake's authority was authentic because it was respectful; it was awesome *because* it was fully human.

The theatrical setting of this story highlights the way aura works. The teacher's teaching happens on stage; it occurs when someone brings the role of teacher to life. As he goes to the microphone at assembly, Mr Westlake finds his bearing and tone of voice change to suit the occasion. He becomes the 'school assembly marshal'. It is not just a matter of deliberate tricks and devices: for a good teacher, the role comes to life, and through his acting, he re-finds his vocation. The role draws on the body, voice, psychology, biography and idiosyncrasies that are present backstage, but these qualities are transformed in the process.

According to Richard Sennett, we must recognise the association of dread with honesty if we are to understand the sort of awe that Michael feels in the presence of Mr Westlake. Sennett distinguishes between the terror associated with a charismatic or authoritarian leader and the awe and dread associated with loving authority. A conductor like Arturo Toscanini, Sennett says, would try to control his orchestra by screaming and stamping his feet and venting his wrath at any player who didn't do as he said. With Pierre Monteux, by contrast, there were no coercions, no threats; he was simply trying to help his players improve: 'Are you sure, cellos, you would like to be so loud?' As part of his kindly and avuncular air, however, Monteux offered the searching honesty of love:

> A moment in the slow movement of the Second Piano Concerto of Brahms when the solo cello is hideously out of tune; Monteux stops the orchestra and looks at the cellist in total silence. What makes it awful is, you know he would never have done this to the last cello in the section; you failed to live up to what *you* should be, and he is calling you to account. And this is again an element in what made Monteux an authority: he had the strength to see through you, to refuse what your peers accepted. (Sennett, 1980: 17)

The charismatic teacher misleads students by encouraging them to be untrue to themselves: they must be as the teacher desires them to be. In some cases, like Toscanini's, this can be terrifying, but, in the case of a teacher who plays favourites, it can be seductive. The loving teacher is dreadful, however, because they demand of students what they know they should have demanded of themselves. They require students to be courageous and true to themselves.

This explains why so many interviewees confided that an element of fear tinged their relations with the teachers who opened their lives. Such teachers are not super-egos, identifying the students' characteristics and judging them against abstract standards. Instead, they are loving and faithful witnesses. Whenever students are inclined to lie to themselves, to withdraw from the world and their own potential, the teachers are there, to call them to account. At the same time, the teachers' sense of wonder and faith is proof to anxious students that the world has an order that offers reason for hope.

School Spirit

When people nominate life-changing teachers, they are often talking as much about the school as the teacher. Miss Vallance and Daneshill were synonymous for Drusilla; Mr Westlake was never Michael Kirby's classroom teacher. These teachers were significant as bearers of school spirit, their aura part of the awe inspired by the school. When Drusilla and Michael felt the spell cast by their teachers, the halls and corridors were hallowed. There was something special here that you wouldn't dream of abusing.

In emphasising the ethos of his schools, Michael was explaining the meritocratic egalitarianism that still guides his life. This is not an imposed obedience, but a sense of dedication and belonging. Michael finds himself by getting out of himself.

> I wouldn't say one [teacher] really stood out. I would say I had evenness of high talent and dedication in my teachers. ... Some were more gifted in communication. But all of them were dedicated and all of them were highly talented. ...
>
> I think what the school contributed ... was a strong conviction about human rationality. And a belief that the world and our country were in a constant stage of improvement. That this was an improvement to which children of parents of relatively modest means, such as those who went to schools like Fort Street, were contributing and were expected to contribute. Not to forget your roots and not to forget that you're one of the ordinary people who happened to have intellectual gifts. That you're not better than other people. That you are a part of the public education in a democracy. It's your duty to try to make your democracy a better one. ...
>
> I learnt to respect the past; but to believe that we had a duty to make things better. ... [T]he emphasis was very

much on public service, political and public life, because there were Fortians who had been on both sides of the political spectrum. Dr Evatt in the Labor Party and Sir Garfield Barwick and Sir Percy Spender in the Liberal Party. ...

I'm going, on the weekend, to Geneva for a meeting of UNAIDS and to Paris for a meeting of UNESCO. I'm chairing both of those sessions. They're part of regular meetings and I've just got to snip them out of my very busy life as Justice of the High Court of Australia. They give me context. I see things in the setting of the world. They're morally useful and interesting and mind-expanding things for me to be doing. So to do that, you've got to just run harder because my life is not just acting and being a judge. It's doing lots of other things which I find rewarding. We were always encouraged.

Michael's life is guided by the sense of service he learned at Fort Street. In serving his extensive communities, he is carrying on the tradition of his school. This was a crucial aspect of Fort Street's expansion of his horizons. The bigger world he entered through school was not simply measured geographically; it was distinguished by a sense of vocation and connection. His school made sense of it for him, making him aware of the responsibilities that put mundane life in hallowed context.

This school spirit has nothing to do with sentimentality or empty symbolism. A school principal may give speeches about the values of rationality, egalitarianism and service, they may make a show of students and teachers being contracted as equal partners, but these words and gestures mean nothing, and produce only alienation and cynicism, unless they emerge from the real life of the school. School spirit does not derive from Gothic buildings, and cannot be instilled through fine speeches; it cannot be effectively simulated through public relations techniques. Even young children see through this superficiality.

On the other hand, the unaffected directness of genuine spirit is equally unmistakable. Parents and students told us that they recognised it immediately they entered the school. One parent said:

> We just knew it was the right school. Prospective students and their families were all in the hall, listening to a speech from the headmistress, when in walked this woman in a toga, covered in tomato sauce blood, loudly warning of the Ides of March. It was the 15th of March, you see. This was totally unexpected, and everyone loved it, and you could see that the headmistress was just as surprised and delighted as we were. That's when we fell in love with the school. It turns out that the classics mistress surprises them with a different Ides of March event every year. The kids adore her.
>
> It's hard to explain what we wanted, though we knew it when we saw it. We wanted more than an academic reputation, though we certainly wanted a sense of academic standards. We wanted a school culture that our daughter could be part of, even if it's not all about good things. You need a spirit that can be part of your memories, so that you're not just at school as an anonymous individual. If a school doesn't have a culture, it's really missing something.
>
> You can see it at assemblies, which are pretty full-on events, with the ritual of academic gowns and the rest. There's lots of recognition of the kids. They're part of the ritual. These rituals can become meaningless and

empty, but not at this school. There's so much vitality. Lots of the girls, after they graduate, come back and help the school in various ways. The sense of commitment stays alive.

Spirit is a guiding force that emerges from wholehearted and responsive relations, from the space between the people at a school. Michael Kirby could only see it incarnated in Mr Westlake because Mr Westlake had the capacity to see it incarnated in him. This aura had an authority that neither would think to abuse.

INTERLUDE

———

Drusilla Modjeska: A Gift for Life

In her interview with us, writer Drusilla Modjeska spoke of the spirit of her prep school headmistress, Miss Vallance. The supportive environment she provided lives on as part of the sense of hope and belonging that sacralises Drusilla's life.

Miss Vallance was the first person who talked to me about going to university. She'd say *When you go to university* … as if she assumed I would. It wasn't a common assumption in those days, and the thought, the idea of it, was sobering and exciting. It gave a pleasurable seriousness to what we were doing at school, as well as the first glimmer of a future that didn't have a shape yet, but to which she'd given this powerful name. It was as if she planted a seed.

Miss Vallance taught history, so it's no surprise that I went on to do history. Or that I became a writer. I learned from her that history is alive with stories, and that within each story are other stories that can change with the perspectives you bring to them. Through her, I discovered point-of-view, that stock-in-trade of the writer, and it fascinated me.

At Daneshill I experienced a world in which reading and thinking and ideas were valued. What she was introducing us to, I suppose, was the life of the mind. She gave us a sense of possibility and an attitude of engagement that we could take with us wherever we went. Nothing need be boring. There was no sense of restriction.

Most of all Miss Vallance had a gift for life. When the crisis of my mother's illness came, and it was time for me to leave Daneshill and go on to my next school, I took something with me that I hung on to. When everything stopped, something remained and it came from her, carried deep inside like a secret map. Looking back, I think that in large measure it was what got me through.

CHAPTER SIX

———

THE PROCESS OF LEARNING

THE LEARNING ENVIRONMENT

Greg Chappell has coached cricket teams at all levels, from school teams to state and national sides. So it may be surprising to hear him say that it is impossible to teach cricket:

> Teaching someone to do anything from a physical or even a mental point of view is quite difficult. In fact you can't teach it. I think all you can do is create an environment where people will learn how to play cricket, and the more fun you make it, the more stimulating it is, the more it gets their emotions, the more likely it is that they are going to learn it.

Greg is insisting that what good teachers and coaches do is create an environment where students can learn. In a sense, then, it is the environment, rather than the teacher, that teaches.

Greg told the story of a sports teacher, a good cricketer herself, who was attempting to *teach* her students how to bat—how to step to the ball, to bend their knees, to put their left elbow up, and so on. Although the advice was technically correct, it had only negative effects on the girls. They were 'tense and frustrated, and they weren't enjoying it because they simply couldn't hit the ball'.

This sort of teaching exemplifies the disconnected experience that Greg describes as 'coaching interruptus'. The teacher, only aware of the students' inadequacies, rushes to correct their mistakes before they have had a chance to learn from them.

> You have got to be able to experience the mistakes. It gets back to the analogy of learning to walk. We get up and fall down, get up and fall down, and the brain starts to work out the balancing mechanisms within the body to allow us to stand up and then to make some progress forward and back and sideways. If we stop kids falling down, then we are interrupting the learning process. The worst thing a parent or a teacher can do is to try and protect the kids from failure, because a failure is a very important part of the learning process.
>
> I think you should set up an environment where the kids will learn and gain experience, and if things aren't working you change the environment to allow it to happen, and let the kids build confidence. But most coaches keep interrupting the learning process. When a coach says *No, no, no, no—don't do it like that, do it like this*, the kid doesn't hear that. What he hears is *I'm no good*. He thinks *I can't do it*. So then the negativity starts to creep in. This form of coaching can be well meaning and you can be absolutely right, but the way you do it can be absolutely wrong. It doesn't mean as a teacher or a coach that you accept less than what's acceptable, but you need to change the environment to allow for some people to catch up while you recognise the ones who need to move on to another challenge. At each stage, you change the environment to produce new challenges.

The interrupting teacher assumes that learning occurs through instruction, a word whose etymology refers to piling up. Instruction is the piling up in students of the teacher's accumulated knowledge. As Greg suggests, this approach to teaching produces a sense of being talked at. Even if they know the correct answers and techniques at a cognitive level, students cannot put them into practice with any fluency. There is a disconnection between the mind and body, the former as mistrustful of the latter as the teacher is of the student.

Greg's point was reiterated by all the teachers to whom we spoke. Deep learning involves discovering an intuitive feel for a discipline—whether it be batting, writing, piano playing or physics—and students will only be able to absorb the teacher's technical knowledge when it connects with this feel. When teachers are patient, and wait for the time when the student can meet another challenge, the knowledge developed is organic and particular.

Rather than pre-empting students' mistakes, teachers create playful environments where students, reflecting on both their successes and mistakes, learn about the game and themselves. Rather than copying their teachers, each student learns in their own way.

Playing with Possibilities

When Greg speaks of *learning how to play cricket*, he connects learning and play. All learning derives from play. Indeed, according to the psychotherapist D. W. Winnicott, all creative life is based on playful experience. Play reduces self-consciousness and generates a condition of relaxed concentration; it encourages an open and experimental attitude to new possibilities.

Greg learned to play cricket through what he calls imaginative osmosis, through playing test cricket in the backyard with his brothers.

They were always Australia versus England—they were the big test matches of the time. Being the older brother, Ian was always Australia, leaving me to be England. ... We would pick our teams and assume the identities of the great players of the day. Ian would be McDonald, Burke, Harvey, O'Neill, Burge, Benaud, Davidson and Lindwall etc., and I would be Cowdrey, Edrich, Graveney, May, Statham, Truman, Locke and Laker, and so on. We simulated the atmosphere of a real test match every way we could, so they were pretty intense games. Of course, we always used a hard ball—Dad encouraged us to do that so we'd get the feel of it. And when you went out, you had to go into the laundry and come back as the next batsman—you actually had to walk off the ground. I can even remember changing the pads, taking them off and putting them back on, and then walking out as the next batter; and if it was a left-hander you'd have to bat left-handed. ... So this is how my cricketing brain was engaged. We were living these moments—they were real test matches—and it was a very important stage in my development as a cricketer. (2004: 73–4)

The point Greg emphasises here is that learning comes from serious fun.

Play is only playful if it involves theatricality. You are playing a part, which in Greg's case was not only the part of a batter or a bowler, but the part of Edrich or Cowdrey, or the part of England or Australia. The suspension of identity is crucial to playing the game. When players become self-conscious or take the proceedings personally, they lose this playfulness. It is impersonality that allows a serious and open-hearted engagement, just as it allows for the element of fun.

To play cricket playfully involves testing out possibilities. Cricket reveals that there is a play or movement in ourselves, in the game, in our relationships, just as there is said to be play in a door hinge. Greg could try being left- or right-handed, he could bowl spin or fast. He didn't need to confine himself to a fixed identity. He could learn and change and grow.

Through the playful testing of similarities and differences, Greg developed an intimate and nuanced knowledge of a whole life. He learned cricket not from an external vantage, but through osmosis. The grace of Greg's action, for example, was a consequence of his learning to play through whole movements. A particular shot flowed from the context of the game. In his 1950s backyard in Adelaide, Greg found that cricket connected him with other times and places. He became the embodiment of the legends and spirit of cricket; he knew Lord's and Old Trafford ovals intimately, while still a schoolboy. Moreover, the principles of good cricket, he learned, were lessons that applied in all spheres of life.

The playful connection between theatricality, analysis and wholeness explains why imagination is one of Greg's key terms. People learn through imagination, he says. Whereas imagination is often taken as a merely mental image, for Greg it is full-bodied and alive.

I must have been about ten and ... I remember watching Lindwall bowl. What struck me more than anything else, apart from his beautifully balanced action, was that he left imprints on the ground where his feet had landed on his run-up. His feet landed in the identical spot every time he bowled. ... I'd never noticed this before. ... I couldn't wait to get home, go to the park, and leave footprints of my own on the grass, just like Ray Lindwall. ... [T]he point was, I wasn't just *copying* Ray Lindwall, I was *being* Ray Lindwall. (2004: 87)

As Greg developed his capacity to learn with bodily imagination, he found that he could conduct practice sessions while sitting in an armchair. These, he said, were as real as sessions in the nets.

Greg's account reinforces the fact that students do not learn by simply following their teachers' footsteps. As we saw with the girls who could make no use of their cricket teacher's technical knowledge, students are alienated by the assumption that learning comes from instruction. Greg's approach to the girls' dilemma was to allow them simply to *play*. He said to them, 'Let's just forget about cricket. We're not going to play cricket today, we're just going to play another game. It will be with a cricket bat and a ball but it's nothing like cricket'.

> I had to get the girls away from what they had been thinking about. So I just threw the ball to them and got them to hit it to a target. All of a sudden, by changing the environment, and by saying *All I want you to do is watch the ball and hit it to that girl, now hit it to this one*; they were just playing cut shots, pull shots, drives, and had no idea what they were doing. I was trying not to let them think about it. And within a matter of seconds in some cases, but certainly within a matter of half a dozen balls, each one of the girls was giggling as they did it, because they could do it. For the first time in their life, they started to hit the ball. I hadn't told them how to hit it. I simply got them to watch the ball and move, and their brains organised the rest. It just simplified the whole process and I think that's so important. They finished up winning every game for the rest of the season and they won their competition.

Just as Greg was Lindwall, and was not just copying Lindwall, these girls played as cricketers, perhaps even as Greg Chappell.

Coaching was not preliminary to becoming a cricketer: the girls learned cricket, deeply and intimately, as they played it.

It would be mistaken to think that Greg's approach only applies to sport. Even the most scholarly activities involve the testing of possibilities. Universities, for example, are institutionally designed to encourage the free play of ideas without which scholarly and scientific work would be curtailed. The notion of play is embedded in the very word 'analysis', which means to loosen. To loosen is to find the room for play, to reduce pressure and density, to enhance fluency and possibility. To loosen is also to lose: analysis is a process of losing our certainties so that we can rediscover how things go together in the world.

LEARNING AS ENGAGEMENT

The anthropologist and systems theorist Gregory Bateson argued that mind is not located in the brain, but exists in relational systems characterised by feedback. 'The mental characteristics of the system are immanent,' Bateson said, 'not in some part, but in the system as a whole' (1972: 287). Mind, in other words, is not separate from the body, and bodies themselves exist as parts of systems.

Bateson offers a useful illustration:

> Consider a man felling a tree with an axe. Each stroke of the axe is modified or corrected, according to the shape of the cut face of the tree left by the previous stroke. This self-corrective (i.e. mental) process is brought about by a total system, tree–eyes–brain–muscles–axe–stroke–tree; and it is this total system that has the characteristics of immanent mind. … But this is *not* how the average Occidental sees the event sequence of tree felling. He says '*I* cut down

the tree' and he even believes that there is a delimited agent, the 'self', which performed a 'purposive' action upon a delimited object. (1972: 288)

Although Bateson's ecological formulation may sound un-familiar, it accords with our most common experiences of being in the world. In Greg's account, the students are learning to play cricket by engaging with the ball. The ball is no longer an external object they think *about*, but something they think *with*: the smallest change in movement from the ball produces sympathetic move-ment in the bat and in the feet, which is readjusted as more infor-mation is received about the effect on the ball of the pitch. This ecological sense of engagement is what is meant when we speak of getting a feel for a discipline, or getting interested in or getting inside a subject.

When we learn things abstractly, knowledge is located in a mind restricted to the self, but learning only becomes deeper, and only becomes full-bodiedly part of us, when it has opened feed-back channels that change our mental capacities by expanding our sense of where and who we are. We do not learn to bat effectively by purposively applying to an external ball the batting techniques we've accumulated in the brain. We learn by becoming cricketers. A cricketer is a different type of being, someone who has learned to let the particular circumstance call out the appropriate shot.

Greg's insistence on the integration of mind and body applies whenever we are engaged in learning. Josie Pellicane is a primary school and maths teacher who offered an example of how she goes about engaging students in maths.

Let me give an example of a Year 3 maths class on shapes. What I might do is put 3-D shapes inside a mysterious sparkly box. I'll capture the children's attention first of all:

What could be in the box? I shake it and they listen. And then different children come and pick out the shapes. Then I'll break them up and they'll have the shapes to play with and measure. Before we start maths with pen and paper, they play and they touch and I let the noise happen too. I think that's very important when they're discovering. And then I am a bit formal; I draw it together so that they come away with something they can clearly say they've got. It ends on pen and paper. I want them to write about what they have done. Maybe I then pick one or two to read out what they've recorded.

How do I know whether students have *got* something? It's definitely body language. You can see a lot through the eyes. And if they're not engaged, the chatter will creep in. I can also tell when they explain it to me in their own words. Or even more helpful, when you see them explain it to another child. That's an exciting moment when you hear them teach one another: *No, it's not like that, do it like this.*

Teachers often talk about the importance of engaging the interest of students, but this can be understood in different ways. Within an instructional model, Josie is 'engaging' the students through props like the box: this holds the student's attention so they can then be instructed. But Josie's lesson also involves a deeper sense of engagement. The box is a theatrical device promising surprise and delight. By inviting students to suspend self-consciousness, the box opens them up and engages them in the lesson. They are curious.

Rather than imparting ready-made knowledge to the students, Josie allows them to use their own bodies and lives as learning tools. In holding the shape, playing with it, they feel its inner form from inside their own. They are engaged, as Josie can see from the aliveness of their eyes and bodies. As she told us, 'When you let an idea resonate, so you truly understand it, it does literally become part of you'. If you learn by bringing the shapes into your being, learning is metamorphosis. For these students, learning about maths involves a change in the world and in themselves.

When Josie gets around to providing a conceptual language, it makes sense to the students because it resonates with their experience. Words allow them to get a glimpse of underlying forms, and to organise what, in a sense, their bodies have always known. A stage is then set for new connections and patterns to be intuited. This is a moment of surprise—of *getting it*—and an opening up of new sets of questions. Such learning isn't the incremental elimination of ignorance, but the interplay of knowing and unknowing. Every bit of knowing allows a deeper sense of unknowing, and it is this revitalisation of wonder that generates the questions that lead knowledge on.

Josie's final step is to allow the students to integrate these intimate and articulated knowledges by finding their own ways to present them. As she puts it, students 'own' the knowledge when they can articulate it afresh, learning through the role of being teachers. Like any teachers, students learn by finding words that fit their experience, and these words, once out in the world, are the nodes from which new connections grow.

Josie has set up the conditions that will bring maths alive in the same way Ray Lindwall's bowling came alive for Greg Chappell. When students are instructed, in the absence of opportunities for play, maths concepts too often stay 'in the head', to be thought about at a distance. Josie's lesson, on the other hand, is designed to involve the whole person—body, mind and soul. Engaged learning is a creative process, for even when it involves the apparent abstractions of maths, students are *living* maths concepts.

LEARNING TO TEACH

Greg Chappell's authority as a coach is crucial to his students' ability to learn. It provides the safe environment where risk-taking is possible. But Greg doesn't think that he can teach his students, he doesn't have a set pedagogic formula that he applies, and he doesn't even know what he is conveying to each student. So what is it that makes Greg a good teacher? The answer is his open interest in what he is doing as a teacher. Greg is effective because he is still learning how to teach. He can never simply repeat a previously successful strategy because each situation will be different. It depends on the particular characteristics and needs of the students.

The flexibility that allowed Greg to find a way through the mental blocks of the schoolgirl cricketers can be contrasted with the self-certainty of the interrupting teacher. The latter is so certain that they know what to do, and simultaneously so afraid they are doing the wrong thing, that they cannot be receptive to students. Greg, on the other hand, approaches teaching with a *What if?* attitude. He tests possibilities as a coach in the same way he tested possibilities as a player, and in doing so he encourages his students to share his curiosity. Teaching itself is a form of play: the unknowing on which it relies isn't a form of ignorance but a willingness to relearn what it knows. Greg's experience tells him that there are always a range of possible approaches and answers, and that failure is not only common, but is the path to learning.

When recalling successful teaching experiences, many of our interviewees recounted stories of how they happened upon just the right strategy for a difficult situation. Anna Eggert, a sculptor and art teacher, told us a story that highlighted the importance of the teacher's openness to experimentation.

I think you have to teach people to find their own solutions and that's the hardest thing on earth. You can only work with the situation and resources you're presented with. I once had a group of students who were in Year 12. They were a bit marginal, nearly failing, and they were offered three weeks of intensive art classes. I got to do that class. I thought *What am I going to do? They will all be rebellious.* I gave them paints and paper and we put it up on the wall and we put plastic on the floor. And the problem was they wanted to make a mess, and you can't make too much mess in a normal classroom. But finally I just said *Do it, if that's what you want to do, and we'll deal with the mess.* And they really got into it and they made a lot of mess and they did some really good pieces. After that, they could actually tidy the work a bit more. They could work from the mess, but they couldn't work from tidy to anything bigger and better. In the end we all enjoyed it and we had an exhibition at the school. I allowed them to be themselves and allowed them to work from their strengths. It's about helping people find their own way rather than lecturing them.

The turning point in this class came when Anna's playful attitude to her pedagogic dilemma allowed the students to set aside their defiance and enter unselfconsciously into the possibilities offered by paints, paper and plastic on the floor. Instead of rigidity, the classroom was characterised by delight and fascination.

Anna's authority as a teacher allowed the students to make a mess without losing their sense of safety and focus. Equally significant, her authority gave *her* permission to play with teaching strategies. She could be flexible, tell herself, 'Let's try this for a class, and if it doesn't work, we'll try something else'. The classroom order made her safe because any failure would provide clues to alternative strategies. If she held her nerve, she would find the way to call out the particular strengths of these students. Her authority and her playfulness, thus, weren't contradictory attributes: they supported each other, just as Mr Westlake's smile and commanding voice did.

BEING IN THE RIGHT PLACE AT THE RIGHT TIME

Drusilla Modjeska told us a story about a student's gratitude. Years after a course, Beth Yahp thanked Drusilla for suggesting she read a book by Maxine Hong Kingston, which had a decisive impact on Beth's path towards becoming a writer. Although Drusilla was pleased that her suggestion had addressed a need that Beth might not have articulated, she was bemused that such a simple gesture could have this effect. It had been offered without pedagogic strategy.

The same imbalance between intention and effect characterises Greg Chappell's coaching. Aware of when students need a new challenge, he offers it by bowling them a different type of delivery, or changing the learning environment in some way. Students find in these situations exactly what they need in order to move on to subsequent challenges: Greg puts students where they need to be without knowing where they are going.

Michel Serres has a word for those who perform this art of placing others where they need to be. They are *préposés*:

> *Préposér:* to put somebody in a position to carry out a function by giving them the means or the authority to fulfil it. … Always present—always and everywhere—when the need of a transformation begins to be felt. Weaving space, constructing time, *[préposés]* are the precursors of every presence. In fact, dare I say it, the préposés are there even before being there. (1995: 139, 146)

This is the logic of teaching in the dark. The miracle is that teachers provide exactly what particular students need at a particular time, without being able to prescribe or predict what the student needed. They can make these provisions because, having faith in the environment created through their authority, they do not interfere by knowing too much themselves, by rushing in with correct answers, by panicking when difficulties arise. By remaining open, they let the environment do its work. In Greg's phrase, the art of teaching is to become redundant. Where once stood a coach, there are now the invisible threads that connect cricketers to their world.

INTERLUDE

———

Shane Gould: Changing Thinking, Changing Bodies

When talking to us, Olympic Gold Medal swimmer Shane Gould was excited about continuing to learn how to swim. The exercises that were inspiring her own training were those she was offering to students too. These exercises are based on the principle that learning to swim involves learning to be a different sort of creature.

At an adult swimming workshop we start by explaining that we are land-based creatures, and when we move into an aquatic environment there will be inhibitions. So that starts people thinking about the basics rather than worrying about the details like *How do I hold my elbow? What do I do to go faster?* People start thinking in a different way and get a bit creative and when they get in the pool they are more open and thinking *Oh that's interesting, I wasn't aware of that before, I didn't feel that, I didn't feel that my legs were that deep or my neck was that crinked.*

One of the main issues we have to deal with is stability: in water you automatically try to create the stability you have on land. So you need to confront that head-on so that people will feel OK about aquatic instability. They need to feel calm, confident and relaxed in the water. So we do various postures and one of these is called the aquatic signature, and it's basically a jellyfish float. You totally switch off, no hands, no legs and you just breathe rhythmically, without moving your jaw. And the longer you stay there the more you turn off. You turn off tension pockets and muscles that are actually holding on to try and hold yourself up and keep you safe. You say *Let go, let go, let go*. It's remarkable, you put them in the water and do a signature, then get them to swim, and a lot of their swimming problems are fixed. Then we might move on to velocity; you need body tone for that. So rather than getting the students to be a jellyfish or a rubber raft, we get them to be a fibreglass canoe or a tuna.

When people are able to apply what they have learned, they've travelled across the silly bridge and back again. The silly bridge is feeling stupid and incompetent and out of your depth. Stephanie Burns says that in real learning you need to cross this bridge with someone holding your hand and then travel back again; and you keep doing that, and then you know that learning involves a change from a time when you don't know something to when you do know something; and to get from one to the other you have to be the humble student.

When my students get cross with themselves, I try to convince them to be patient. I ask them questions: *What are you experiencing? Why are you feeling this way? What were your expectations?* Because it's different for different people, some people get it and have the great experience straightaway, and for others it takes a month before they become more body aware or shift their thinking. People become defensive when they feel overwhelmed. They get jaded, they get this glassy look in their eyes, and you know it's time to stop or to change tack.

CHAPTER SEVEN

———

DIALOGUE AS AN OPENING
OF THE MIND

The Meeting of Difference

Interest, engagement, wonder, fascination, curiosity, inspiration and relevance are all forms of encounter, meetings of differences. Dialogue takes the same form as these meetings. It is inherently educational because the different experiences of the interlocutors reveal different aspects of the world; moreover, knowledge is revived and reformulated through this re-contextualisation.

When we say that learning is dialogic encounter, we are not only talking about relations between people. The student alone at a desk with a book is in a relation with that book. The young students playing with three-dimensional shapes are in relation with those forms. The awareness of the element of difference is the basis of both relationship and the ability to learn. This point was made by the sculptor Anna Eggert when talking about her relationship with different materials.

> I find that clay doesn't offer enough resistance, but when I work with stainless steel, it's so hard that I feel I can be more aggressive towards it. It's got its own surface and its own character. If it can offer me a resistance we can work.

I really need to dominate it and I need it not to be dominated, so we have to come to some kind of balance! A meeting, so we can do things. I sometimes talk to my material in my studio; I say *We can do this! Work with me!* I hope nobody hears me! I can listen to what it's saying in response, but not always; the more frustrated I am, the more I don't listen, which is so counterproductive. I've been known to sit there and cry because it just wouldn't do what I wanted. But once I've been through that, I start again gradually and then I can usually get back into it. After the crisis I can let go of my need to control, and the work that follows is often really different; it's a different level of work.

The learning that takes place in these encounters depends on the creative openness of the relations. The opening of the mind is openness to larger systems of relations, in the terms of Bateson's ecological theory of mind. To get inside the knowledge you must get inside the book and the shapes and the steel, and allow them to live inside you; you must relearn who 'you' are by acknowledging how the other connects with you. It must be a meeting, as Anna says. Collaboration isn't just a useful teaching device and isn't just a skill to be taught because employers value it. Learning *is* collaboration: a respectful collaboration involving students, teachers, texts and the forms of the world. What we know and how we know are issues of ethics and values.

People often assume that the 'di-' in dialogue refers to *two* parties, in contrast to the one party of a monologue. This misunderstanding highlights how difficult it is to escape identity logic. In fact, 'dia-' indicates *through*. The logic of dialogue is relational, and not based on exchange between two prior and identifiable positions. The point is well made by the physicist David Bohm, who believed that everyday dialogue was based on the same principle as that of the universe, the unfolding of potential. Reflecting on a weekend seminar devoted to these themes, he said:

> The weekend began with the expectation that there would be a series of lectures and informative discussions with emphasis on content. It gradually emerged that something more important was actually involved—the awakening of the process of dialogue itself as a free flow of meaning among all the participants. In the beginning, people were expressing fixed positions, which they were tending to defend, but later it became clear that to maintain the feeling of friendship in the group was much more important than to hold any position. Such friendship has an impersonal quality in the sense that its establishment does not depend on a close personal relationship between participants. A new kind of mind thus begins to come into being which is based on the development of a common meaning that is constantly transforming in the process of dialogue. People are no longer primarily in opposition, nor can they said to be interacting, rather they are participating in this pool of common meaning which is capable of constant development and change. In this development the group has no pre-established purpose, though at each moment a purpose that is free to change may reveal itself. The group thus begins to engage in a new dynamic relationship in which no speaker is excluded, and in which no particular content is excluded. ... [G]oing further along these lines would open up the possibility of transforming not only the relationship between people, but even more, the very nature of consciousness in which these relationships arise. (1985: 175)

Dialogue, then, is not based on interaction, competition, opposition, exchange or the reconciliation of positions, for all these conventional logics imply the persistence of individual selves and distinct positions. Instead, dialogue implies a *new kind of mind*, a dialogic form of consciousness that isn't located in any or even in all of the individual participants, even though it operates through them. Within a dialogue no one possesses knowledge, but all participate in it. The implication of this is, as Bohm points out, that knowledge is infinite because it is always unfolding.

LISTENING AND QUESTIONING

Socrates insisted that he was not teaching people but engaging in dialogue with them, only asking questions of himself and others. Unlike the schoolmaster's question, which is disingenuous because the teacher already knows the answer, the Socratic question is raised from within the ongoing dialogue. By listening attentively, the teacher hears a possibility that hasn't yet been drawn out from what has already been said, and offers it to students in the form of a question.

Sharon Cheer's description of her mentor, Alison Pegus, gives a good example of how dialogic learning functions in an everyday class working through a prescribed curriculum:

> Alison was not just listening for the sake of listening, but really listening to understand what's going on for that child. And she chose really challenging material for them. She [taught] a Year 4/5 class called 'Family Groupings' and she did a unit on genes and the natural world. Natural selection, all this really rich learning. And these girls, who were quite capable, they just lapped it up. And if you had said *I'm going to talk about Darwin's theory with a Year 4 class*, people would have said *No way*. But Alison could do it,

and the girls felt excited to be involved. She was very good at questioning, an exceptional questioner, and she would challenge their assumptions on everything, keep questioning, keep digging, keep digging, keep digging. So she really got deep, getting them to explore their own assumptions and the assumptions of the theory. I suppose Alison modelled for me how to guide children to come to their own conclusions rather than telling them what to think.

Let's imagine this classroom dynamic. In preparation for the class, the teacher will have made a class plan. After familiarising herself with the whole topic, she will have imagined it from the perspective of the students and developed an accessible pathway through the topic. She will have turned the steps on this pathway into a series of varied activities, to allow students the chance to feel their way into the issues. The focus provided by these activities is crucial: the teacher will want the students to have the chance to concentrate on particulars, and not feel as if they have to grasp everything at once. Likewise, the module structure gives the teacher the possibility of focus: she knows that there will be regular chances to take stock as the class proceeds, to adapt plans in response to feedback.

As the teacher introduces the first class, the students will be curious and available, like a theatre audience. The teacher may have in mind a sense of what she wants to get across in the class, but she will be patient, not offering too much material at any one time. Her emphasis will be on getting a flow of discussion. Rather than trying to tell the students what they need to know, she will be giving them ideas and materials that get them going.

When it comes to be the students' time to talk, the teacher listens closely, in a way that allows her to feel what is going on for them. She's as interested in their tone and gestures as in their words. And instead of rushing to align what they say with what a textbook might say, she empties herself of what she consciously knows and allows the students' words to work on her—to call out possibilities. It is these possibilities that she reformulates as questions. The most apt questions emerge from the most interested listening, and not from a sense of where the discussion should be going if it is to arrive at the right conclusions.

The teacher's manner is so open and curious that students don't doubt the value of what they have to say. There is no feeling that the teacher is trying to get a correct answer from them. But the teacher's queries have suggested new connections and given the students fresh ideas, and they answer each question openly, following it wherever it takes them. This is the process of challenging that Sharon mentions. It isn't a testing of the students, but a testing of possibilities: Could it be that …? So is it really true that …? The teacher's manner here will be reliably persistent. As Sharon puts it, Alison would challenge their assumptions on everything, keep questioning, keep digging, keep digging, keep digging. This process keeps students open to the implications emerging in the dialogue. It challenges assumptions and keeps ideas in play. As implications are drawn out, the ideas become more enmeshed in the students' lives, and the knowing becomes deeper, more relevant and more alive. The students are changed.

When the discussion reaches a certain fluency, the teacher can inconspicuously remove herself in order to allow the students to realise their own dialogic capacities. By using her authority, she can break the ice, helping students past their shyness with each other. Sharon Cheers talked about the importance of the teacher getting out of the students' way:

> One of the ways I encourage acceptance of differences
> is a little strategy called Two Before Me. It's like peer
> tutoring. If they say *Oh I'm really stuck on that*, I say *Well,*

So and So is really good at that—go and ask them. And you just keep modelling that. First, it's really good for your classroom management if they're not always coming to you, and second, you can create that culture of asking each other.

I think it's valuable to position yourself as not always having the answer. I think that's an ego thing and some teachers can't let go of that. I don't think those teachers ever get the true experience. It's something you see with having prac students. I had a supervisor who came out and said to a prac student *Yes, you've told me all about what you're doing, but what about the children? What are they doing?* I thought it was a brilliant question. I suppose it's the phase of development too because you're so worried—*Am I doing the right thing? Am I doing the right thing?*—that you can't focus on the students' needs.

As Sharon implies, an inexperienced teacher may be so incapacitated by their sense of responsibility that they cannot take the risk of openly responding to students. Faced, for example, with an unresponsive class, such a teacher may be too embarrassed to ask why the lesson isn't working. A good teacher, on the other hand, finds no discrepancy between the two senses of responsibility. Having made careful plans, she is confident that the dialogue will be productive, even if it doesn't go as anticipated, even if the approach has to be changed.

The good teacher's plan allows her to wait patiently until the dialogue reminds her unexpectedly of points she had intended to make. Had she wilfully inserted them into the discussion, they would have obstructed the flow and the students' creative potential. By waiting, she has allowed students to encounter an idea just when they needed it and are able to accommodate it. At this moment it *makes sense*.

When they are engaged in this way, students are listening with the interest that allows them to formulate their own questions on the basis of what the teacher and other students say. They are, in other words, performing a teacher's role. Their questions to the teacher, for example, are likely to draw out the teacher's thinking. As a teacher told us, in every class she gains new perspectives from 'the interesting places where the students' questions are coming from', and she has to think afresh in order to answer such questions. The student who sees this is encouraged by the proof that what they say matters. A sense of confidence comes from the difference they make to others.

In this situation, other opinions are not experienced as threats but as invitations to play with new ideas. What one student says about family likenesses gives another student a sudden insight about similarities between species. Students' self-consciousness is reduced as it becomes clear that no one has the last word. The ideas of genetics meet the lives of each student, but each student finds their own particular resonances.

When Bohm talks about a 'new kind of mind', then, he isn't referring to a uniform group-thought. The friendship he refers to doesn't require people to adopt a party line. The dialogue stays alive because each participant connects with what others say but connects differently. The theatrical or conjectural element in dialogue enhances curiosity by diminishing the need for personal defences: there is always more to learn from others.

Both students and teacher are excited by this dialogue. It feels alive and important. They are aware of how much they've learned because the class has developed through the very process of unsettling presuppositions. While a teacher may bring the threads of such a dialogue together at the end, the class doesn't conclude with a sense that all the questions have been answered. Indeed, classes that work like this have become unafraid of open questions. Students have learnt that the well-judged question is the basis of knowledge. Good questions manifest deep understanding, they crystallise what is known in a productive tension with the unknown.

Just as Greg Chappell's students became cricketers in the first hour, Alison's students have had first-hand experience of the serious fun of scholarly dialogue. Like Greg's students, they have discovered that this learning process never ends.

THE UNKNOWING OF TEACHERS

When describing the attributes of their favourite teachers, people invariably emphasised their teacher's inspiring passion for a subject. This passion implies that the subject and the teacher's life are indivisible. Since the teachers live and breathe their knowledge, there is no possibility of the external vantage point that would let them see the total scope of their subject. There is no final way to say what is known, for knowledge is continually being reformulated as life offers new connections: knowing and unknowing augment each other. This is why passionate teachers are so vibrant.

When Nick Jose talked about his teacher, he emphasised the depth of knowledge that Mr Schubert brought to the classroom. Mr Schubert, on the other hand, emphasised the importance of his unknowing. In a letter to Nick, he said:

> No lesson in which I didn't learn as much as my class was
> of any value. To me teaching something was by far the best
> way of learning it. Now often I found that my knowledge
> of a work—an ode of Keats, a play of Shakespeare—which
> I had long been familiar with was only a glib one. And
> certainly a class would find you out. No amount of study,
> of course, would unravel *Lycidas* or *The Ancient Mariner*,
> but all that was essential was the plain evidence that you
> had grappled with it. I also fancy a teacher is fortunate

above most because he has the privilege of encountering so many minds vastly superior to his own. Together they can engage in that one essential pursuit of man—endlessly to seek out the truth. As Donne puts it *On a huge hill, / Cragged and steep, Truth stands, and he that will / Reach her, about must, and about must goe.* Except for those blinding moments which fire you to continue the search, there is, of course, no hope of ever attaining your goal. And beware of that man who claims he has done so. But, as I see it, nothing exonerates one from this unrelenting task.

As knowledgeable about literature as Mr Schubert was, it was his childlike wonder and delight that allowed him teach. He was an exceptional teacher because he was an exceptional learner: the deep form of knowing that teachers need is characterised by a simultaneous unknowing. To allow new connections to emerge from classroom dialogue, teachers must hold lightly those that they have previously made, allowing their knowledge to re-form around new starting points that arise in the class.

This unknowing, Kym Lawry explained to us, is a matter of trust. Teachers must trust that the whole of their experience will be evident in their response to whatever particular points arise:

You need to be open. I suppose having been confident in my physics and confident in the faith students have in me, I don't feel threatened. Some classes work really well, students are prepared to ask anything. You don't know what the magic is. I've had classes where the whole year progressed through their questioning. It's unbelievable. One of the joys of teaching, I suppose, is to be part of that open part of their life. Because they're really open to ideas, I'm learning too. There's a sense of wonder. The mixture of that inward turning on themselves and having the ability to look outward as well.

Over the years I have become more confident about being open-ended, less constrained. Previously in practical classes, I would have given them a sheet explaining what to do, step-by-step instructions—very structured. What we got was students following a recipe, doing what they're told and getting the answers. Now I'm more likely to say *Here's a pendulum. Make it swing back and forth. What are the things you can find out about this? Investigate it.* We do more and more of our instruction like that. It's much more valuable when you can use the students' experimental desire. *Think of a question first.* We specifically assess that. Have they come up with a good question? You're teaching them about analysis. What you want students to do is open up to asking bigger questions than how the pendulum goes back and forth. The essence is to give them the tools to ask questions. This is much better preparation for exams and also for the rest of life.

Teachers share their openness and love of learning, but, rather than sermonising about these virtues, they perform them, *with* students. They model openness, but, crucially, they do not put on an external display of openness. Indeed, were they to attempt such a display, they would distance their students, turning them into spectators. Students learn from inside the model, from their own participation in the openness.

When students see their teacher's wonder, they recognise that wonder is what they too are experiencing. When they see the teacher's excitement about learning, they recognise their own excitement. And in these moments of recognition, students *feel* what they see: they know their teacher's excitement from the way they feel, and they recognise that their feeling is excitement from the way the teacher looks. This is what Kym means when he refers to *the mixture of that inward turning on themselves and having the ability to look outward as well.* This is a self-knowledge that remains open: students are coming to know themselves relationally. They experience their potential, their fluent whole.

This is a new stage of maturity in the learning process. While everyone has experiences of creative fluency, we are initially too immersed to gain a reflective understanding of them. They are even difficult to remember because they are unwilled and unselfconscious states. But when these states are witnessed and affirmed, we both experience *and* witness them. The *wow* of wonder that comes to accompany them is a crucial sign of this awareness. It allows us to recognise, understand and trust these states; it allows us to see how relations carry us.

Winnicott insists that these experiences are the ways in which people learn how to live a whole and open life:

> [I]f someone is there, someone who can give you back what has happened, then the details dealt with in this way become part of you, and do not die. ... That is, the sense of self comes on the basis of an unintegrated state which, however, by definition, is not observed and remembered by the individual, and which is lost unless observed and mirrored back by someone who is trusted. (1991: 61)

Just as the students' enthusiasm gives the teacher confidence in the value of their lessons, the teacher's state of wonder gives students confidence in their capacities. Moreover, they see that their value isn't just in giving the correct answers or displaying correct behaviour. The more questions they ask, the more risks they take, the richer the life of the class becomes. They learn that, as Greg Chappell put it, 'an open heart and an open mind is all you need to reach your full potential in life'.

Good teaching, then, is a demonstration of how to hold questions open and take discussions further. This demonstration is the deeper lesson at work in any classroom dialogue. It is a lesson that doesn't draw attention to itself because it is a performance in which students are fully involved. In learning about the world with their students, teachers teach students how to learn. They show them how to enter into lively relations, and how to be more than they could be by themselves. In this way students learn how to enunciate ideas that are theirs but which they couldn't have spoken or even remembered by themselves.

FEEDBACK

A relational view of education highlights the organic possibilities of feedback. Whereas feedback is commonly understood as an external form of evaluation, every response and every recognition in a dialogue is feedback. Feedback is a moment in the life of a system that doesn't demarcate boundaries between inside and outside. It allows the development of a dialogic consciousness that suspends the desires and defences of self-consciousness and thereby opens the mind.

To illustrate how feedback holds the learning process open, here is Anna Eggert's account of her relation with her art teacher, Deborah Singleton. Like all students, Anna often desired the safety of completion, but Deborah's trustworthy feedback allowed her to find a more open sense of satisfaction in the creative process itself:

> Deborah and I really connected. I thought she was understanding what I was trying to do rather than what I was doing. When her casual position lapsed, I got in touch with her and asked if she could occasionally give me a bit of feedback. I think what she did was listen to me for long

periods of time. She didn't try to set her agenda onto me, she let me go, and in the end we kind of communicated.

With art, there's an internal struggle. You're grappling with things that are not yet visible and when you grapple with them for a long time you think they are visible and you think *That's really good, I can see it*. And then Deborah would come in and wouldn't see it and I'd think *It's not there, is it?* I couldn't believe it: the whole thing collapsed. I had to get outside myself to see what was really there. And then I could do more with it.

For example, those works up there, when they were in their early stages they didn't float off the wall. When Deborah came to look at them, she didn't say *What's wrong with these?* She asked, *How are you hanging these?* And we looked at the back and I said, *They're a bit flat on the wall, aren't they?* I think she put her finger on the way the work related to the wall, and once I saw that, I thought *Yeah, that's the problem!* And then she helped me find the solution—went on the journey with me.

There were other teachers, though, who put their agendas onto us. They'd give you a lecture on Lacan or Baudrillard. It was useful because it pushed me on to do more reading, but at the time it withheld me from my work. I suddenly felt inadequate; I felt the big theory should be there; I felt I had to fulfil someone else's interests. But then the work couldn't come from the heart.

Deborah allowed herself to hold a condition of unknowing. Because her questions arose from a feeling that wasn't forced into definition, they were not designed to lead Anna to an answer that she, Deborah, already knew. When Anna saw the unease on her teacher's face, she could recognise her own submerged feeling of unease—could acknowledge the problems that she had not been facing because of her desire to finish the work. When acknowledged, each blockage became an organic way forward.

By contrast, the art theorists couldn't offer genuine feedback because they were too preoccupied with their own theoretical interests to see the work itself. Had Anna followed their advice, she may have received praise, but her work would have been removed from the wellsprings of her creative potential.

In today's popular terminology, Deborah *facilitated* Anna's learning and her creative process. Facilitation is often seen as a non-confronting laissez-faire process of letting students do what they want, but, as we can see from Deborah's feedback, a more complex and edgy process is involved. Since students' self-centred desires block their work, teachers facilitate by using their authority to help them get *outside themselves*.

Imagine being Deborah. Anna's expectations could have imposed a demand that Deborah accept the work as completed. To challenge this expectation was to risk facing Anna's disappointment and resentment. It would have been easy to try to please Anna, but such a response would have been insulting to their relationship. Deborah's priority as a teacher was to serve Anna's potential rather than falsely protect her self-esteem. She had to challenge Anna's comfortable assumptions in order to keep her real and to keep the working process open.

This courage is only possible if all partners in the school community respect the teacher's authority. A parent talked about the impasse that arises when the authority of teachers is unrecognised:

> Parents can overreact because they want to protect their children from risks. It must be hard for teachers sometimes: I can imagine them feeling that they're facing a flotilla of anxious, over-ambitious parents. And they sometimes react to this pressure by trying to soften the blow, trying to reassure the parents about the child's progress.

Maybe these days they're also worried that if they point out the children's problems, these will be seen as problems caused by them or the school. So they can be a little bit glib in their feedback, not getting to the heart of things. But parents and children need to know where the weaknesses are and what can be done about them.

Teachers who provide open feedback *both* make a decisive difference to students' work *and* allow them to develop their own work. This is not a contradiction, but an unfolding of the logic of the I–Thou relation. Whereas the usual model of facilitation assumes that learning is self-expression, a dialogic understanding allows us to appreciate that facilitation is a matter of relational change. Both students and teachers are involved in the relation and changed by it. Each facilitates the other through the mutual modelling of a relationship.

ASSESSMENT AS FEEDBACK

One of the ways teachers provide feedback is through assessment that is not treated as an end in itself or as a simple ranking mechanism, but as part of the learning process. Although students have an understandable anxiety about assessment, they look forward to the challenge offered by creative assignments. This pleasure derives from their relation with teachers. As a parent told us, her children see their work as a gift to the teacher, and they wait in pleasurable anticipation for the teacher's response:

Getting written comments makes a big difference; they take it to heart, reading the teacher's comments carefully. They don't just say to me *That was a good mark and comment*. They consider the comments and do things with them. Especially if they have done a big assignment, they wait for the teacher's response. That's what interests them, not the mark, even if it is 10 out of 10.

The teacher's response to an assignment is addressed to this student alone, setting challenges that are developmentally within their reach. Another parent made a special point of this in her interview:

What students need is guidance; they want to do well, but they don't know what 'well' means or what this piece of work means about them or their other work. My son, for example, he's only in primary school, but his favourite teachers are the ones who ask the most from him, who know the difference between his good work and his careless work. He takes it, I think, as a mark of respect. But the suggestions need to be specific or the kids don't know what matters. For example, if teachers don't comment on grammatical mistakes, students won't understand that grammar is important, and they won't develop an ability to pick up these mistakes themselves. They need to be stretched. That's how they develop.

Major assignments are a rite of passage, the culmination of a particular stage in an educational process. They give students a chance to focus their resources and see what they can do with what they have learned, to assess the creative possibilities emerging from their relations with their work. Because they have reflected on the strengths and weaknesses of their work and their working process, they are prepared to receive the teacher's feedback. This highlights the intimacy of this process. The teacher's comments bear witness to the vulnerable moments when students were alone with their work and their hopes and fears. Assessment takes classroom dialogue to another level by offering feedback on the students' own feedback systems.

Students find their work rises to a different level when addressed to teachers they trust and respect. Students know that teachers will know if the students have not stayed open to their work and honest with themselves, and it is the teacher's responsibility to recognise these qualities. Scattered through the work will be inspired passages that call for the reader's response: *Something inspiring occurred to me here: do you notice the difference? Does this work for you too? Should I persist with the risk of working openly?* Aware of the importance of these questions, good teachers know that students will know if they have been less than fully present in their responses.

The intimacy of this relation transforms assessment. What could have been a mass process becomes a sensitive encounter in which students are heard respectfully. They discover that what is most their own is also what is most valuable to others.

INTERLUDE

David Ritchie:
Talking Directly to Students

David Ritchie is an actor, director and a teacher of performance studies at university. We spoke to him because of his interest in the connection between play, participation and learning. David insisted that in both teaching and acting, engagement comes from unmediated communication.

Apart from providing a map of the territory, lectures are there to enthuse. If students don't leave the lecture enthused about something they haven't quite understood, then the lecture's failed. That's why you have to talk to them. A great discovery you make with Shakespeare is that a lot of Shakespeare is designed to be talked with an audience. That teaches you a lot about lecturing. I mean if Claudius does that inner monologue *O my offence is rank it smells to heaven it hath the primal eldest curse upon't a brother's murther!* the audience can't hear it. But if you look directly at the audience and say

> O my offence is rank, it smells to heaven;
> It hath the primal eldest curse upon't,
> A brother's murther!

then you're using time, and time is absolutely important. You're contacting the audience, you're checking all the time: *Is this being understood? Is there a dialogue?* And you know, if you get a nod or a response. And lectures have to be like that.

Voice is interesting because it's almost unmediated communication. If someone screams in pain, it's like an electric shock: it doesn't get processed, you know it instinctively. Often as a director I say to actors: *The voice is what you actually touch the audience with—not the words carried by the voice. The vocality is an immediate communication of your physical state and with it you can touch, you can caress, you can slap, you can nudge.*

CHAPTER EIGHT

PLAYING YOUR PART

Part and Whole

A relational or dialogic pedagogy avoids the polarisation of canon- and student-centred approaches to learning. In a dialogue, we learn about a topic by engaging with it, learning about ourselves as we learn about it. There is no contradiction between student development and curriculum content because they draw out each other's implications. Because dialogue removes self-defences, students are free to learn openly, from a direct encounter with the content of the lesson.

When discussing play, we insisted that students learn by participating in the worlds of cricket or maths or art. Through being a part of that world, students gain an intimate knowledge of the whole; participation changes their sense of time and space so that they are no longer subjects looking at distant objects. When Greg Chappell, for example, was playing fluently, he embodied the whole tradition of cricket. He was simultaneously the Australian test captain playing in Brisbane, a young boy playing in an Adelaide backyard, Ray Lindwall playing at Lord's. Whereas self-defences stifle fluency, unselfconscious actions take place in a here and now that connects with the whole. Greg's fluent drive was both timeless and perfectly responsive to the state of this particular game, both classic and unmistakably his.

To see how the logic of parts and wholes operates in academic disciplines, consider the examples of history and anthropology. Students *get* these disciplines when they see that in studying others they must reconsider their own place in the world. History and anthropology don't just tell students how people used to be or how distant societies are: they show how humanity *is*, in an eternal here and now that connects here and there, now and then. Both disciplines are forms of participant-observation. If we take this logic a step further, we see that it applies to all sciences. Biology, for example, teaches students of their creatureliness and their ecological embeddedness. When students engage with something other than themselves, they are changed by seeing their lives in a new context. High-school physics teacher Kym Lawry explained:

> Kids want to find ways to live their lives, and it's hard because we live in a secular environment that encourages self-absorption. When they find things to look at outside themselves, and have a wonder about the world, they see a reason for engaging with the world. One way of having engagement with the world is to look at it through a physics perspective. There are some amazing perspectives and insights you can get from that. People often tell one story, use just one lens for looking at the world, but there are others you need to engage with. I love looking at it through a physics perspective. I think I give students a sense of enthusiasm about physics.

INITIATION TO MYSTERY

Explaining how Mrs Miller taught Shakespeare through class performances of the plays, Julie McCrossin recalled how effortlessly student- and canon-centred approaches came together. Through these performances, Shakespeare came to life for Julie. She still feels his plays in her bones, his words trip off her tongue, yet she is still learning their meaning. 'The spirit of the canon', Julie said, 'is alive and well for me'.

When identifying the basis of Mrs Miller's approach, Julie talked in terms of faith and mystery. Mrs Miller believed that if she brought her students into the direct presence of Shakespeare, the plays themselves would transform their lives: 'At heart that's because Mrs Miller believed that great works of art have a mysterious power'. Julie illustrated this mysterious power with a story from her own life.

> I was in the kitchen and some music came on ABC FM and I listened to it, really listened to it. I remember sitting on the kitchen step with tears pouring down my face, I was just so moved. I discovered later that it had been sung in English, but because it was opera I couldn't understand the words. It turned out that it was Yvonne Kenny singing from *Dido and Aeneas*. I quickly wrote this down and rang up a friend, who explained that this was Dido's lament, sung just before she puts herself on the pyre. It was amazing: what an amazing achievement that it had communicated to me its substance without cognitive understanding. That's art! If one day I play that to my stepdaughter I will be curious to see her response to it, and I will trust in its power. If she doesn't respond now, I know she will later. I'm patient, because I so deeply believe in the thing. That's the faith that Mrs Miller had too.

Julie is focusing on the magic of great art, but she could equally be talking about the beauty of mathematics, the grace of cricket or the wonder of science. Passionate teachers gain much of their authority from having been touched by these mysteries, but what they know is the experience of mystery itself. Teachers cannot turn this experience into a finite content that can be conveyed to students—Mrs Miller could not explain the mysterious power of Shakespeare any more than a mathematician could account for the beauty of a proof—and yet whenever teachers speak with resonance, and whenever they act with love, they are drawing out the implications of this mystery. They teach, then, not as the masters but as the devotees of mystery. Their pedagogic responsibility is not to instruct but to initiate students, encouraging them to give up previous ambitions and certainties and to follow mystery themselves. These teachers have faith in the magically transformative power of education, knowing that the power isn't theirs.

When Leslie Devereaux talked of the high-school teacher who most influenced her, she spoke as if he were a shaman and education, a rite of passage. He seemed to have initiated her into her vocations of anthropology and psychotherapy.

I went to a public high school in a small, Midwestern city that has no particular distinction or aspirations. My English teacher in my senior year was a lover of culture, and he and I just clicked at that level. He had a mysterious air. He loved words and loved getting us to think about words. Once, he set a kind of mysterious project which none of us understood—he had given us clues and bits of paper and objects—and I remember giving up on the possibility of getting it right. I was very anxious initially, and annoyed, because I was used to being the top student, but he cut across achievement issues and turned it into a creative undertaking.

He had a twinkle in his eye. He was the kind of man who could hold the class's attention. He took himself seriously in the sense that he took the act of living seriously and I think his authority came from that—there was something about him. I don't remember him foisting anything on us, but his love of things kept spilling out, his passions. I remember 1963 and the *Lord of the Rings* had just arrived in the States, and he came up to me one Friday in class and pushed a book towards me: *I have a feeling you might like this. If you do, there are two more and when you finish this one you can trade it in for the next one, if you like.* I went home and read the first story and it was magical. It was enticing and mysterious. He was inviting me to take an interest. Something in his character was saying *Yes*, with a kind of twinkle. And he had a long-term effect—I followed mystery in that sense.

To follow mystery, Leslie had to let go of self-certainty. She remembered her teacher's project because it made her realise that she valued mystery more than the pursuit of answers and top marks. When students read for answers, they read fearfully and self-consciously, on the outside of the text looking in. But when students have faith, they find themselves in the place where they can be moved by the text's mysterious power. Not knowing where the text is taking them, they take their reassurance from the joy of the reading process.

It is the teacher's authority that allows students to develop their faith in mystery. English teacher Barbara Devlin called attention to the importance of this faith when describing a poetry lesson for Year 10 students, many of whom were 'really terrified' of poetry. Rather than choosing a poem she knew well, Barbara chose one that she found intriguing. She had been moved by it but didn't quite know why. Having told the students that the poem was new to her too, she put it on an overhead projector and they worked through it together.

I'd be underlining and saying *I don't know what that means yet, I don't quite know where it fits*. And kids would be saying *I like that bit* and I'd ask them why they liked it and *Does anybody have a different bit?* and between us we worked through it. In some ways it might be quicker to say *I am going to do this annotation for you*, but that's not always effective. My approach is to give kids the confidence to agonise, to make sense of what they're reading, and you can't do that just reading out of a book. It never ceases to amaze me: you think you've covered it all, but there are new interpretations and that is part of the beauty. And I have no shame in saying to a kid in the class *You know, I haven't thought of that before. That's fantastic. I'm really interested*. I loathe the word 'facilitator' because it denigrates what teachers do. I might not be dictating to students, but I *am* teaching them.

Barbara's faith in what she doesn't yet know gives the students confidence in their capacity to engage with the poem until something emerges. Because the poem's mystery takes the students out of their comfort zones, it allows them to see unrecognised elements of their own lives. The distinction between inner and outer worlds is unsettled in such a reading process. As the literary critic Hélène Cixous put it, it is the strangenesses in any text that catch our attention and reveal our potential. 'Texts are the witnesses of our proceeding. The text opens up a path which is already ours and yet not altogether ours.' (1988: 148)

This faith in texts is simultaneously a reader's faith in their own ability to openly meet a text, face to face. Understanding occurs when a text means more than the reader can say, yet allows the reader to continually discover and articulate its potential meanings. This is an intimate process of a text and a life growing together. Faith is not a trust in an outcome but a commitment to mystery.

LIVING TRADITION

Our interviewees continually remarked that Shakespeare was the heart of their education, and the teachers nominated as life-changing were disproportionately those who used classroom performance to introduce students to his plays. Losing his distant and iconic status, Shakespeare became a witness and guide in their lives. David Ritchie, actor and teacher, insists on the importance of this 'constant discovery through performance':

> I've always found that if you give students a task which involves intellectual and creative input, it releases an enormous energy usually. If you work on a text, if you perform a text, if you embody a text, then you see the life of the words, you see the life of the structure, you see the skill behind it. Shakespeare's the obvious case in point. He was himself an actor and one of the things I'm interested in is his theatricality. Everyone always concentrates on the drama, the poetry, the Bard, but if you get the theatrical point of the scene, it comes alive. So you need a hands-on experience to discover that [clicks his fingers] moment.

While some teachers approach Shakespeare through an interpretative grid (Leavisite, post-structuralist, feminist, post-colonial and so on), David believes that when students participate in a play, the whole text comes to life through them. It is no longer a re-enactment, a re-presentation. Shakespeare is a real presence, alive now. The education is not in working out what Shakespeare 'really meant', but in discovering Shakespeare as he allows students to re-discover themselves.

This participatory pedagogy changes the way that instruction is used. David demands, of course, that his students do extensive research about Shakespeare, his times, the different theoretical approaches to Shakespeare, the history of performance, and so on. He gives background lectures to map out these territories. 'Ideas and theory can be really important because they can take you to places that you wouldn't otherwise get to.' But the aim of this instruction is to enthuse students and loosen their minds. Once the facts have been mapped and the theories discussed, and once the lines have been memorised, students are encouraged to suspend what they know and trust that they will rediscover its relevance through performance, now in an infinitely more lively form.

Although all educators value students' familiarity with their cultural heritage, there are different ways of understanding this familiarity. A cultural work studied like a museum piece on a pedestal is not the same as one that is allowed to reverberate until its significance sings. The former appreciation will be dutiful but will not touch us: the object of appreciation is something from the past. The latter is visceral and shocking: the past is here now, demanding our response.

The sudden coming to life of a work is exemplified by David's response to a performance by his students.

> Even when I am teaching I am discovering. For example, a group of students from China did a piece from *The Seagull*, which I'd coincidentally seen the week before. Chekhov calls *The Seagull* a comedy. The students' English was not perfect but they were doing a good job. I said to them, *It's actually quite funny, go for the comedy*, and it was hysterical, hysterical! They did it in a heightened style. One of the student's mothers actually works for the Peking Opera and she'd got at that style. I went *Yes! Chekhov can work like that!*

David was familiar with *The Seagull* and familiar with Chinese opera, but his epiphany made a new connection between them. Suddenly he saw possibilities of form in both Chekhov and Chinese opera that he hadn't seen before. Sometimes these moments feel as if they are of earth-shattering significance (*Ah! So that's it! Now I get it!*); sometimes they are the little sparks or clicks of connection when things fall into place (*Yes! I hadn't seen that before! This fits with that! That's what they meant!*); but always epiphany is a transformation of time. It comes as a moment of awe, suspended from ordinary clock time, taking place in a zone where past and future meet to make sense of each other. We have an uncanny sense of seeing something for the first time, yet having known it always.

Learning, then, isn't simply a steady accumulation of knowledge. When we *get* something, knowledge that we don't even know we've acquired is suddenly recalled through its connection to the present situation, and we see potential in it that we hadn't seen before. So, as Thomas Aquinas put it in the thirteenth century, education is the never-ending actualisation of potential. Past and present bring each other alive in the eternity of the *Yes!* of understanding.

According to T. S. Eliot, an education without this sense of universal time is without courage or depth. Education, he says, only fulfils its promise when it brings tradition to life.

> [Tradition] involves a perception, not only of the pastness of the past, but of its presence; the historical sense compels a man to write not merely with his own generation in his bones, but with a feeling that the whole of the literature of Europe from Homer ... composes a simultaneous order. This historical sense, which is a sense of the timeless as well as of the temporal and of the timeless and of the temporal together, is what makes a writer traditional. And it is at the same time what makes a writer most

acutely conscious of his place in time, of his contemporaneity. (1951: 14–15)

Eliot's argument has implications for the selection of educational texts. Only texts that have a sense of both the temporal and the timeless are open to meetings, for without the mystery of tradition there is no space for creative reading.

So what do people mean when they say that studies must be relevant to students? A complacent interpretation of this in literary studies is that students should study contemporary novels about the problems of adolescence, or read Shakespeare's plays in terms of topical issues of our day. A deeper sense of relevance arises when the encounter with Shakespeare changes our sense of who we are. Understood thus, relevance is not based on sameness but on a recognition of difference, even our difference to the person whom we thought we were. Relevance is not a confirmation of the student's existing identity but is the shocking rediscovery of our world.

Although tradition is often considered conservative, and can be, it is never so with good teachers. In keeping the canon alive, these teachers open students to mysterious, disturbing and unconscious cultural forces. Literary critic George Steiner refers to these forces as 'real presences', and describes encounters with great works of art as annunciations that break into the small house of our cautionary being. Any work of art asks 'What do you think of the possibilities of life, of the alternative shapes of being which are implicit in your experience of me, in our encounter?' And, Steiner concludes, 'If we have heard rightly the wing beat and provocation of that visit, the house is no longer habitable in quite the same way as it was before'. (1989: 142–3)

Steiner's annunciation image reminds us that education is creative, a matter of inter-being and begetting. Necessarily life-changing, it is a risky process that is neither controllable nor predictable.

Unique Contributions

Advocates of student-centred learning are concerned with the unique contribution of every student. Without a relational pedagogy, however, uniqueness can be misunderstood. Rather than an expression of autonomy, uniqueness is the particularity that comes from participation in a whole. It derives, as Eliot says, from being part of an unfolding community:

> I think of literature ... not as a collection of the writings of individuals, but as 'organic wholes' ... There is accordingly something outside of the artist to which he owes allegiance, a devotion to which he must surrender ... in order to obtain his unique position. ... Between the true artists of any time there is, I believe, an unconscious community. ... The second-rate artist cannot afford to surrender himself to any common action; for his chief task is the assertion of all the trifling differences which are his distinction: only the man who has so much to give that he can forget himself in his work can afford to collaborate, to exchange, to contribute. (1951: 24)

If people have tradition in their bones, they are no longer writing or reading as distinct individuals: through lively relations, they are creating more than they could have done on their own. Their uniqueness emerges not from self-expression but rather from this mysterious *more than*.

Students who treat schoolwork as self-expression are left feeling overwhelmed, since tradition has already claimed the best lines: how can they find anything new to say? What these students don't realise is that their problem is pride rather than inadequacy. The teacher's task is to help them see that the tradition will enable them to say what they need to say.

Mr Schubert offers a case in point. When Nick Jose had become a successful author, he wrote to his old teacher, mentioning self-doubts. Mr Schubert responded by reminding Nick that, because of his calling, he had no choice but to participate in the tradition. In keeping the tradition alive, Nick would necessarily be changing it in his unique way:

> And now you have become a writer—lucky you. I suppose the problem is how to make the language of the tribe, which is the only one available to you ('What no one with us shares, scarce seems our own'), the medium of your own unique individuality. What fascinates me are the interstices of language, the meaning that pulsates between the words, the saying of what is not being said, of what cannot be said, of what is unsayable.
>
> We'll have to forgive you what is surely only a momentary heresy—'The world may not need another book' you say. But, as you well know, of course it does—if for no other reason than because it's a different world from what it was a moment ago, and with the passing of that moment, the whole past has shifted, so that Dante, for example, now means something else than he did before.

Mr Schubert's gentle rebuke must have made Nick smile with recognition, for Mr Schubert's life and teaching was a warning against the vanity of treating writing as self-expression. Insisting on close, respectful relations with texts, Mr Schubert cautioned against displays of cleverness, whether they be claiming the definitive understanding of a text or the invention of a novel interpretation. Nick told us of his gratitude for these lessons:

> I learned to read literature from him, a way of reading that was close, sensuous and very precise. This subtle way of

responding is what I still use when reviewing something or writing something myself. I feel quite confident in my method; I can trust my responses and I can articulate them. I don't need to try too hard, but just do it naturally as I've been taught. I know it will work: I proved that to myself with Mr Schubert, who wouldn't let me get away with showing off. When showing off, you're interposing your own bright ideas, rather than letting your responses come from the text.

Mr Schubert taught that unique work comes from love rather than self-expression: if Nick engaged open-heartedly with language, his work would always be original, a revitalisation of the old in the new. A writer's calling is a sense of what the tradition calls for: the tradition needs the writer's participation if it is to unfold unique aspects of its potential.

PARTICIPATING IN LIFE

> But Death, alas! I cannot shun;
> Death must come … (Dido, from *Dido and Aeneas*)

Students who learn through participation are being initiated into life's mystery. Greg Chappell's awareness of the cycles of past cricketers showed him that he is part of a tradition, that he is the bearer of a game that has a history and a culture, a game that has its own seasons and evolutionary process. For someone who loves the game, cricket is not a self-centred activity: you are doing your part for the game before you too pass into history. A lesson in cricket is, as Greg insisted, a lesson in life.

In a participatory approach to teaching, then, students' knowledge grows as they grow, and students grow by finding their place in the cycles of life and death. When students are interested in their studies, they are aware of their implication in a whole. They are learning to deal with birth, love, sex and death—the universal, yet intensely personal, issues of our creatureliness.

Vicky Yannakouros was alluding to the importance of the bigger picture when she said that her kindergarten classes involve talking, talking about everything. Covering the curriculum topic of 'living and non-living things', for example, Vicky's dialogic method allowed the students to ask such questions as *What does living mean? How are people made in tummies? Who was the first person in the world? How did monkeys turn into people? How did the caveman get alive?* These universal questions about the cycles of life arose from the students' particular concerns. This is an awesome meeting, as Vicky recalled in relation to another such discussion:

> It was a really fascinating discussion on the adoption of Vietnamese children into Western families. I remember going home that night and thinking *Oh my God. This is the first time they've probably confronted that whole issue of a parent choosing to give away a child, and they talked about it with me. I hope I did it justice. I hope I did it fairly and honestly with them.* You want to expose them to everything, but you hope you're not preaching. That would be dreadful. But to share experiences with them, that's just so exciting. It's just beautiful.

When education involves these lessons in life, the idea of relevance takes on a deeper existential significance. High-school teacher Judith Moreland-Mitchell gave the example of teaching *Hamlet* to students who had neither a background in religion nor direct experience of death. Finding that they didn't understand the significance of the Last Rites, she shared with them her 'experiences of death, the dramatic change that occurs once people have been given the Last Rites and have accepted that they are going to die'. When you teach *Hamlet* in this way, it is no longer just words on a page, she said, but real death and real life. 'I think you can really make them stop and think, and they appreciate that.'

A work like *Hamlet* is canonical because it is universal, dealing with the life and death issues that Judith calls religious issues. Its mysterious power is that any reader will be able to find in it the most profound concerns of their own life. Julie McCrossin told a story to make this point. She had recently interviewed Paul Brock, a senior educationalist, who was diagnosed with motor neurone disease eight years ago. Now Paul can move only his neck, three fingers on one hand and one on the other.

> He's written this marvellous book where he asks, how the hell do you accept the unexpected? His book and the interview were sprinkled with references to Shakespeare and Ecclesiastes; he had quotes from the absolute mainstream canon which spoke directly to his circumstances. It's the great works that provide guidance and succour in a way that, no matter how entertaining, popular culture never can.

One of Paul's favourite quotes is from *King Lear*. When he first read the play he couldn't have imagined that one day he would see himself as Lear lost in the storm. But these days, trying to understand his own predicament, the words of Lear's Fool give him counsel:

> He that has and a little tiny wit,
> With hey, ho, the wind and the rain,
> Must make content with his fortunes fit,
> Though the rain it raineth every day.

In his adversity, Paul has found what he needs in the tradition to which he belongs. By giving voice to the truth of Paul's condition, the tradition includes and shelters him, just as the Fool does Lear. Paul feels heard and un-alone.

If these issues of mortality are difficult for everyone, they are particularly so for adolescents, who often imagine that safety will come through self-assertion and achievements. The alternative safety provided by teachers allows students to gradually acknowledge their limitations and mortality. Rather than being independent agents, they realise that they are playing a part in continuing and in revitalising a tradition that will outlive them. Just as the formality of Mr Schubert's classes allowed Nick Jose to come to honest terms with his sexuality, it allowed him to come to terms with his place in literature. He learned that he didn't need to show off in order to feel special, that a devotion to writing and reading is more joyous and engaged. In teaching Nick how to read and write, Mr Schubert was teaching him how to live; in teaching the curriculum, he was offering pastoral care.

The value of these lessons is often brought home to people when their beloved teachers die. This is the teacher's parting gift. Keenly aware of both the loss and continued presence of their teachers, students understand that in living well, they are keeping alive their teacher's spirit. Thus, teachers who may have sought no honours for themselves find immortality through the work of their students. One of the speakers at a memorial service for Mr Schubert was John Bannon, former premier of South Australia. To conclude his tribute, he quoted the words that Mr Schubert had himself used forty years before in his memorial to another teacher:

> He was one of those who, serving the school with complete devotion, gave not only what he had but what he was, and his character and personality have been built firmly into the fabric of the School.

———

Greg Chappell:
The Ability to Reflect

Greg Chappell emphasised the importance of developing resilience, an ability to learn through internal feedback. Such awareness allows you to recognise when you're not fully engaged with the task at hand.

It's in learning to deal with failure that you start to build some resilience. And the further you go, the more failures you are going to have. What I have found through my sporting career is that it isn't the most gifted ones who succeed. It's the ones who learn about themselves best, learn the coping skills, learn to recognise the danger signs and the good signs, and learn to manage their way through the obstacles that life presents.

The turning point came for me when I developed the ability to reflect on myself and my game. I woke up one day—thankfully early enough in my international career, I would have been about twenty-two—and realised that I had all these coping skills and I had all these concentration processes that I didn't even know I was using. It was only when I sat down and reviewed all the games that I'd played that I realised that on the good days I did things that I didn't do on the bad days and vice versa. So I learned that I needed to be aware of my thought processes and my emotions; I had to be aware from the minute I woke up in the morning of what my mental environment was like. Was I in the right frame of mind to be able to succeed? When batting, the most important thing was not to get distracted, not to get ahead of myself. Don't worry about the ball that had just been bowled, don't worry about the one in the next over. I had to focus on the ball that was being bowled to me right now.

When I started reflecting on my game, I realised that I'd been using concentration skills but only on an ad hoc basis. So I developed a routine for before and after every ball and that was what allowed me to concentrate for hours on end. I worked out in my layman's way that there are three levels of concentration. There is a level where I'm aware of what is going on but not seriously involved. Then there is the fine focus where I start to concentrate on what I'm involved in. Then there is the fierce focus when the bowler bowls the ball. For the split second that it takes to get from his end to my end the only thing in my field of vision is the cricket ball leaving the bowler's hand. I have to cycle through these three levels. The routine allows me to relax in the awareness level—I might count the fielders or look to where my family or friends are sitting—and that gets me ready for the next ball.

CHAPTER NINE

———

A FULL LIFE

LEARNING FOR LIFE

The best teachers teach their designated subjects by way of lessons in life. When genuinely engaged in their work, students find their lives through the subjects they study, and the subjects through their lives. In learning, and in learning the basic skills that learning requires, they are learning how to live.

Shane Gould:
Some teachers only teach a technique, but a good teacher shows how technique is part of a way of life.

Vilma Rotellini:
I'm not just teaching the language, although that's part of it; we're trying to help them respect custom, tradition and difference.

Diana Doherty:
To put it simply, it's teaching them how to grow through this example of looking at one thing, the oboe, specifically.

Kym Lawry:
In all aspects of school life, inside and outside the classroom, the teacher is teaching a way of being that is caring
and compassionate and enthusiastic. You're teaching
people how to respond to different realities.

Greg Chappell:
You can only learn to be a champion cricketer if cricket
is teaching you about life. I am a committed learner for
life. Everything I have learned about cricket has helped
me learn about my off-field life, and what I've learned off-
field has helped me with cricket.

These comments indicate the variety of meanings in the
expression 'learning for life': learning as guidance on how to live
well; learning as a life-long process; learning as an enlivening
experience; and learning as responsibility, as the student's particular
contribution to life. In any one of these meanings, all are implied:
learning is a mode of being, a way of life. Learning, as a meeting
with difference, is awareness of being alive.

Learning for life challenges the common view that education is
a preparation, that adulthood and real life begin when education
has overcome ignorance and dependence. From a relational view,
maturity is neither knowingness nor independence, but a capacity
for open relationship. Maturity is the awareness that mortality connects people with cycles of life that are not theirs to control; it is
the awareness that original work comes not from self-expression
but from devotion to a calling. With wisdom, as Serres says, people
realise that they are always just beginning to learn.

Children think it's important to be big and grown-up, and
some adults, if they've never grown up, think the same.
There they stand, as cardboard puppets, or wax dummies.
The process of growing up involves the discovery that the

little ones—the *préposés*—so pliant and mobile that they seem to have wings—are more important than the big ones, stuck in their posedness. (1995: 148)

The immediacy with which people talk about their teachers confirms that they never leave them behind. Their teachers are still with them today, in the studio, on the stage, or, in Michael Kirby's case, in the court:

I'll always be grateful to my teachers. I remember them like a rosary (even though I'm Anglican). I go through them seriatim. I go through each one of them. I remember each one of them quite vividly. They're not forgotten in my mind. They're clattering around in my brain. They were great influences in my life.

In talking this way, our interviewees didn't mean that they had simply adopted the teacher's admirable qualities and followed their good examples. What matters is their *ongoing* relation. As Michael recounts the teachers' names, he reflects on his life: *Is he serving the community? Has he been honest with himself? Is he living up to his potential?* One by one, in their different ways, the teachers raise the questions that help him appreciate the world he now faces. As he changes, he perhaps comes to appreciate lessons he hadn't previously understood.

Michael's story shows that maturity is neither dependence nor independence. He is alone when reflecting on his teachers, in the same thoughtful condition he is in when writing judgements or speeches, but this condition is not isolated. When he works by himself he works in relation with himself and in relation with his work. He can draw out his thoughts because, in this psychic space, he is both teacher and student; he can be creative because his education has taught him how to 'internalise' a dialogic pedagogy.

DEVELOPING A HOLDING CAPACITY

It is the teacher's capacity for reflexive dialogue that allows students to develop their own maturity. As Leslie Devereaux explained, students learn how to hold conversations and hold their desires and anxieties because they have experienced their teacher's holding capacity:

As you work as a supervisor you encounter in trainees upsets and locked-in positions that are resonant with your own. And you meet that and say *Yes, I can usefully hold something of that.* In supervision I'm watching someone go through a learning process. I'm holding their anxieties and their joys of discovery, and I'm holding my own as well. I don't want to make the trainees feel wrong, so in order to find a way to articulate something of what I'm hearing, I might say *You know what I'm wondering here?* I will try to raise it so it's just a potential meaning that they can pick up at that moment or not. They can only pick it up when they're ready, otherwise they're just being obedient.

In being a teacher with a student, or a therapist with a patient, what we create in our relationships is the state *between* our worlds. So when my patients or students come into my office, we form a relationship. We can feel it around us. My thoughts go into that space and their thoughts can go into that space and we can feel that mutually. And then in that space something else happens, a dialogic thing as it were.

When Leslie talks about *holding*, she refers to the teacher's capacity for the patience and tolerance that suspend her desires. She is fully involved in the relation with her trainees but with an equanimity that doesn't get caught up in their upsets and positions. In holding her own anxieties, she is holding the students'. She is also careful to avoid any conclusive interpretations, knowing both that the students must discover what it is that they need to learn, and that she too will learn from the dialogue. In holding her conclusions, she is holding the conversation.

By alleviating the need of students to affirm *locked-in positions*, Leslie helps them loosen the grip of their identities and come into relation with their desires. Realising that their positions had been unnecessarily constraining, students become aware of the unreal fears on which desire is based. They become aware too of capacities they didn't know they had. As they relax, they see that they also have the capacity to hold the conversation so that it is effortlessly creative. This awareness is a vital stage in the development of maturity.

To explore this developmental process further, we'll consider Guy Hungerford's account of his art lessons. Just beginning his career as a university tutor, Guy wants to develop the holding capacity that he experienced with his teacher Jane Wisner.

> This probably sounds melodramatic but I think Jane taught me to be a human being. Before I met her, I was very anxious, very, very needful of control. I'd separate myself from other people, or from situations, and close in on myself. These lessons were the first chance I had to open myself, to really trust other people and to relax and allow myself to enjoy the warmth of being around others without worrying about who's winning or trying to impress myself or others.

Guy told us that the more he tried to be in control, the more frustrated he became. The fantasy of getting it right made him so fearful that he was unable to sustain a working relation: his art was a lifeless attempt to find and erase mistakes. Jane's lessons taught him to be a human being because they showed him how to stay with his work, and with himself, in an I–Thou relation. She taught him to be patient and tolerant.

> I remember sitting on the floor of her studio with my piece of paper and there'd be something in the middle of the room that I was to draw. Jane was generally off to one side and she was drawing as well. Because I was completely focused on the drawing, I could feel her presence but I wasn't particularly conscious of what she was doing. It didn't feel like someone watching every stroke of my pencil. I could do what I liked, but she was there as a supervisor, or guardian, a kind of safety net, so that if I went too far off the track there'd be someone who'd shepherd me back. It was amazing how focused I was on the drawing. I'd just get lost in it.
>
> I'd had this experience of concentration before, on my own, but being in that classroom helped me to sustain the feeling. When I was drawing on my own there'd be some detail that I couldn't get right and I'd get frustrated and I'd just walk away. Whereas when I was drawing with Jane and I got stuck, she'd suggest something like *Just leave that alone for a moment and work on something else.* She'd notice I was having problems even before I got really frustrated. Occasionally I'd ask for help, and she usually gave the same advice: *Don't worry about it now, it's not important.* After a while with Jane, I began to develop more patience and an ability to relax and stay with something. When problems come up, just keep drawing. Let the solutions come from the rest of the picture rather than try to pull it out of myself.

With the quiet presence of a shepherd or guardian, Jane transformed Guy's experience by holding it in an I–Thou relation.

With Guy, she produced a space where neither felt the need to identify what was theirs and what was the other's, a potential space where Guy could easily uncover possibilities hidden from his controlling mind. A problem at one point of the page would dissolve when it revealed the potential of another point of the page; no longer finite and external, what he was drawing would express itself through him.

Guy's light awareness of Jane is like that of a young child playing in the presence of an unintrusive mother. According to Winnicott (1990: 30–4), this is the situation in which a capacity to be alone develops. When we are alone we are in the presence of someone else, someone who guards us but who doesn't need to interfere.

It was Jane's maturity that provided Guy with the supportive environment he needed to develop his awareness. She was not preempting Guy's process or trying to express herself through him. Instead, her own drawing kept her relaxed. She looked at his work through the soft and curious eyes that looked at her own page. Teaching is a form of art: Guy and Guy's drawing and Jane and her drawing were all developing together, but in their own particular ways.

COMPASSIONATE AWARENESS

To be alone is to have a reflexive relation with yourself that is often called awareness. Whereas Guy's attempt at independence relied on a controlling I–It relation, awareness is based on a compassionate I–Thou relation. It involves witnessing yourself with mercy, rather than observing yourself with judgement; it means having a relation with your failings, fears and wounds. Anna Eggert described it as the continued presence of her teacher: 'I find I ask myself those questions that she would have asked. It's as if she's standing above my shoulder, helping me develop my work in a way that I want to develop it'.

Awareness, then, is the mature capacity for reflexive dialogue. Just as ordinary dialogue allows students and teachers to find inspiration through each other, the solitary worker finds inspiration through awareness of their own otherness. Moreover, this awareness is developed through ordinary dialogue: the holding space of dialogue creates a meta-system through which people receive and respond to their own feedback.

Diana Doherty described her education in terms of the importance of developing this compassionate relation with herself. When she began her oboe lessons overseas, she was often paralysed by self-criticism. The turning point came when, talking with a friend, she became aware of the psychodynamics of her playing. She could see the harmful effects of self-criticism, but she could also sympathetically understand the neediness that underlay perfectionism. With awareness, Diana learned to be alone with her instrument; things that she once would have regarded as mistakes became moments of interest: *What happened there? Does that tell me something about my breathing? What would happen if I changed my posture?* This curiosity also changed Diana's relation to perfectionism itself. She learned to treat symptoms of intolerance as useful warning signs; by withholding judgement she could wait until the symptoms redirected her to the love of music. Maturity came, she told us, when tolerance and curiosity transformed perfectionism from saboteur to guide.

Compassionate awareness not only teaches Diana how to play, it teaches her how to teach:

> I've done a lot of work on myself, addressing my perfectionism, and building a healthy confidence rather than being so critical of myself. This has helped me understand other people. Because being alone in a room with your instrument makes you confront all your imperfections, understanding how you relate to the world is the most

important thing. So what I'm doing in teaching is helping a student to develop a way to deal with themselves. Some of these people will not go on to be professional musicians but hopefully these skills will be useful for them, not only in the musical context, but helping them analyse themselves without putting themselves down.

Diana can help students develop a relation with their issues because she is, as she says, holding her own demons. She teaches students by teaching herself in their presence. This is not a modelling of excellence; she is not perfect, she is real. It is awareness of vulnerabilities that allows Diana to be open to her students' potential.

As you become more mature, and learn who you are and what you can do, you become more able to focus on other people rather than seeing everything through the veil of your own insecurity. I think too that aside from teaching, what's really important for me is that I always want to learn, I always want to know more, I always want to get better as a person. I want to be a good example to students of how to be and how to live and so I think, the most important thing, if I'm teaching, is that that doesn't stop me learning.

PRACTICE

When Diana talked to us, she used the word practice in two different ways. Early in her career it was a means to an end; now it is a musician's way of life, a discipline that has no end. If learning is a way of life, practice is a devotional ritual, an everyday service to your vocation. It is a word, like 'passion', 'enthusiasm' and 'inspiration', that carries deep religious resonances.

While maturity is the continuation of classroom dialogue after graduation, practice is the continuation of the order provided by classroom routines and rituals. The patience that allows things to happen at the right time is learned through the rhythms of the school day, the slow and precise reading of a literary text, the steps by which you gradually unfold a maths problem. Josie Pellicane was touching on the real value of homework when she remembered the pattern it formed in her life:

> I remember Kate Skrzynecki getting us to write sentences at night in Year 2. Mum tells the story of my just sitting and revelling in that—writing words and sentences. She would be in the kitchen and I'd write them up and then rattle them off to her. Mum said I loved doing this, it wasn't onerous. It was reassuring and nurturing to know that Kate would set that homework and give us feedback. There was a routine in the day and in the week and that was calming.

The ritual element of a working process holds students, slowing time and allowing them to be fully engaged. Ritual is a form of flow. As Diana insisted, it is through practice that work develops grace and fluency.

> One of my early teachers said it was better to practise as if you did not expect to get to a destination. That changed the picture in your mind and changed what you produced. Before that I would have practised for an hour and thought, *I've practised for a whole hour, how come I can't play better yet?* I'd be really down on myself and frustrated and I'd just want to go and watch TV.
>
> Students are often told that there's good practice and there's bad practice but I tell my students that any contact

with the instrument is better than watching TV. The frequency of the contact is at least as important as the quality of the contact. By encouraging regular practice, I help students develop a healthy relationship with their instrument and themselves. If they expect perfection every time, they won't practise.

I'm happy even with postgraduate students to sit down and look at their timetable and work out a practice program, because I think that routine and structure in one's day really helps. It keeps the mood healthy and positive; it keeps you focused on what's important, and it removes anxiety and guilt about when to practise. If I don't have a routine I get into an anxious state: I've got emails to answer, faxes, letters to answer, phone calls to make, and so I'm anxious because I want to practise but if I practise and I haven't done those things then I can't concentrate on my practice, but if I do those things and I don't start practising until 11.00 then my mood starts to go down because I'm already feeling guilty suddenly, so it just never gets done. But if you always do the same thing more or less every day you know where you are. I have breakfast at 8.00 and then I practise from 8.30 until 10.00 and then I'll go out and see what I'll do with my day. I feel more comfortable if I've got that practice under my belt first. I can say *Look, those things can wait, I've just got to practise.* And then I'll feel much more confident talking with these people.

Like the bells in a monastery, Diana's timetable calls attention to the part of life that matters now, promising that there will be time later for the other aspects of her life. There is a time for dealing with emails and phone calls; there is a time for students, and a time for the family. Her practice is a way of life, the connection between different parts of life. Because these aren't competing, they can refresh and augment each other. Rather than feeling fragmented, Diana feels the whole of her life in each part.

Maturity, then, is the capacity to live in time. It is the skilful ability to be present and empty, the patience that allows time to unfold. As David Ritchie told us, this maturity allows us to recognise newness in every repetition:

> I have found the more experience you get as a performer, the more you realise the value and mystery of time. We tend to think spatially and visually; language is just full of visual metaphors and it's very poor in temporal metaphors. So when you have the practice and skill to go into something that works in the dimension of time, you are constantly discovering something mysterious and wonderful and terrific. It is a fascinating dimension—stillness and time are very powerful.

Through practice, David can lose his self-consciousness. Entering the life of a play, he brings the play to life, speaking and moving with a rhythm that is just right.

A FULFILLING LIFE

Throughout this book we have drawn attention to the relational logics on which good teaching relies. The good teacher has faith in, and knows how to serve, classroom relations. Moreover, as Kym Lawry told us, what teachers know of service is ultimately the main lesson they offer students:

> I don't denigrate exams. Students have to do them. But that's not the most important thing in life. I'm passionate about teaching physics, but a physicist's view of the world

is just one part of the story. It's a nice coherent story, but you have to say *Look, physics offers one way of looking at the world, find some others. Find something that excites or engages you. You have to do more than just survive, get a house and a car. You have to find meaning.* That's why my involvement in the school is wider than physics. For example, I've run trips to Samoa where we've got involved with primary schools and Australian Volunteers Abroad.

In a wholistic sense, my role as a teacher is to play a small part in equipping students to become successful humans. What you're hoping to do is help them become happy, positive, enthusiastic, committed, just, engaged members of their society. I want to show them that there are lots of different ways in which they can be involved in life and make a contribution. This is not old-fashioned charity, but a sense of responsibility: *What's your response to the world?*

Students whose lives are most whole and most fulfilled will be those who become most engaged with their work, with other people, with the world and with themselves. Whether in school or outside it, engagement is the way to learning and learning is the development of engagement. By engaging with *other people's realities*, we learn to draw out our own potential and become most fluently and creatively ourselves.

This responsive ethics makes sense of the lessons that Miss Craig taught Betty Churcher: a rewarding life comes not from ambition or self-assertion but from a wholehearted devotion to whatever you are doing. Betty said,

I've never had a career plan, I've never been ambitious. But when opportunities have come to me, in true Miss Craig fashion I've given them all I've got. That was what she was on about. She said that empty vessels make the most sound, that if you're trying to promote yourself, you'll fail. But if you try to promote what you're doing, you will float up with the success of whatever that is. That's what I got from her.

Miss Craig was a very good leader. I suppose it's a bit like a conductor of an orchestra or a director of a gallery. You don't put the exhibition together yourself, but it's your enthusiasm, your willingness to help others that makes it happen. I felt as a gallery director that you have to set the tone of the institution, and that's what Miss Craig did. By setting the tone, you let the staff work to their capacities, and the more the staff do, the better the institution becomes. I think Miss Craig and the school were very well respected in Brisbane, because she had such a good staff and good students.

Miss Craig was drawing attention to the difference between the fragmentation of career and the wholeness of vocation. Whereas career involves a narrowing of interest, calling is necessarily educational and enlivening because it is a response to the world. Because she can respond to different aspects of the world, Betty is aware of her own complexity. Just as the various parts of the world connect, so do the parts of Betty's life; just as each part of the world is important to the whole, so is each part of Betty's life. Her life has been full because it has been, like Miss Craig's, a life of service. In nurturing the potential of others, Betty has done things she could never have done on her own.

According to Buber, the magic of life comes from 'each mortal hour's fullness of claim and responsibility' (2002: 16). Life is full when you attend openly to what is at hand, whether it is the report you're writing, the concert you're listening to, the food you're preparing, or the person whose needs call to you. The teacher's ultimate responsibility is to help students find this meaningfulness.

Good teachers leave no identifiable mark on their students—they do not *direct* them—but they are present whenever students feel that, through their vocation, they belong to the world. Teachers are the spirit that animates their students' lives.

REFERENCES

Bateson, G. (1972), *Steps to an Ecology of Mind*, Frogmore: Paladin

Bohm, D. (1985), *Unfolding Meaning*, London: Routledge

Buber, M. (1958), *I and Thou*, New York: Scribner's

Buber, M. (1966), *The Way of Response*, New York: Schocken Books

Buber, M. (2002), *Between Man and Man*, London: Routledge

Chappell, G. (2004), *Cricket: The Making of Champions*, South Melbourne: Lothian

Cixous, H. (1988), 'Conversations' in Sellers, S. (ed.) *Writing Differences: Readings from the Seminar of Hélène Cixous*, Milton Keynes: Open University Press

Eliot, T. S. (1951), *Selected Essays*, London: Faber and Faber

Emerson, R. W. (n.d.), 'On Education', The Works of Ralph Waldo Emerson, <www.rwe.org>

Gaita, R. (2001), 'The Pedagogical Power of Love', Keynote Address, Victorian Association for the Teaching of English, 4 May

Gaita, R. (2004), 'Love and Learning and Realism', Keynote Address, Australian Catholic University, Sub-Faculty of Philosophy and Theology, Teaching and Learning Symposium, 14–15 April

Sennett, R. (1980), *Authority*, New York: Alfred A. Knopf

Serres, M. (1995), *Angels: A Modern Myth*, trans. F. Cowper, Paris: Flamarion

Steiner, G. (1989), *Real Presences*, London: Faber

Thompson, P. (2004), *Wisdom Interviews: Betty Churcher*, Radio National, ABC

Winnicott, D. W. (1990), 'The Capacity to be Alone' in *The Maturational Processes and the Facilitating Environment*, London: Karnac Books

Winnicott, D. W. (1991), *Playing and Reality*, London: Routledge

INDEX

T

Y

Yannakouros, Vicky: biographical
note, xxvii; establishing feeling
of safety, 75–6; importance of
bigger picture, 144; I–Thou
relationships, 36–40; letting go

at end of year, 29; love in
education, 35–6, 37–9; respect
for children, 39–40; teaching a
love of learning, 54–6
Yes!: 'getting it', 64–5, 104; of
understanding, 139